Copyright © 2015 by Charles O. Young, Ph.D.

Intentional Evangelism

by Charles O. Young, Ph.D.

Printed in the United States of America
ISBN-13: 978-1514734698
ISBN-10: 1514734699

All rights reserved solely by the author. The author guarantees all contents are original and do not infringe upon the legal rights of any other person or work. No part of this book may be reproduced in any form without the permission of the author. The views expressed in this book are not necessarily those of the publisher.

Unless otherwise indicated, Bible quotations are taken from The New King James Version of the Bible. Copyright © 1982 by Thomas Nelson, Inc.

Contents

Prologue 5

Think Intentionally 7

Testify Intentionally 13

Teach Intentionally 18

    Make it Evangelistic 22

    Everything Rises and Falls on Leadership 24

Talk Intentionally 80

Plan Intentionally 87

Fish Intentionally 94

Intentionally Drawing the Net 111

Pray Intentionally 116

Conclusion 119

Prologue

"Sometimes we don't need another chance to express how we feel or to ask someone to understand our situation. Sometimes we just need a firm kick in the pants. An unsmiling expectation that if we mean all these wonderful things we talk about and sing about, then let's see something to prove it."
                                                                                    --Dietrich Bonhoeffer

Has the Western Church lost its way in personal evangelism? Perhaps not totally, but it can certainly be said that it has cooled off. Around the world, evangelism seems to be running hot, especially in the Far East. China is reaching people in record numbers, such that there are more believers in China than in the United States. This is all done without the permission of the Chinese government. In fact, the explosion that is taking place in China is being met with great opposition. It may be that the "Church" does better in the area of outreach when it is under persecution.

Within the Muslim world, a Muslim is accepting Jesus every 15 seconds, according to some reports. Of course, within the Muslim world, it is very unpopular for one to become a follower of Jesus. In fact, to do so causes one to risk his life.

The United States is in a rapid moral decline. Christians seem to have chosen the path of criticism instead of evangelism. Most believers have fallen to "cursing the darkness" instead of being "salt and light." Criticism does not change a person's heart. Only Jesus can do that. Of course, some believe that the moral decay is in itself a form of persecution. They even gloat that they are so much better than the decaying world, yet never take credit for the decline. Rather than lamenting the world's condition, it would be more effective for followers of Jesus to attack the source of the evils, and acknowledge it as spiritual. If every believer would exercise his responsibility to the command of Jesus to win the world, the moral tide would rise. When the tide rises, all ships rise.

To date, the Western Church is not experiencing persecution. If persecution drives evangelism, as it seems, the American Church must draw on other catalysts to help it be motivated to introduce lost people to Jesus, the only answer to the ills of the world-- physical, social and spiritual.

The purpose of this book is to help with this motivation by suggesting that a follower of Jesus could become more intentional in their approach to fulfilling the Great Commission.

Think Intentionally

"Five percent of the people think; ten percent of the people think they think; and the other eighty-five percent would rather die than think."   *--Attributed to Thomas A. Edison*

You are the only person who can tell you what to think.

This is an important statement as it proves true in many areas of our lives. The Apostle Paul tells us in Philippians 4:

> *"⁶ Be careful for nothing; but in everything by prayer and supplication with thanksgiving let your requests be made known unto God. ⁷ And the peace of God, which passes all understanding, shall keep your hearts and minds through Christ Jesus. ⁸ Finally, brethren, whatsoever things are true, whatsoever things are honest, whatsoever things are just, whatsoever things are pure, whatsoever things are lovely, whatsoever things are of good report; if there be any virtue, and if there be any praise, think on these things."*

These verses are all about what you think. If you think about bad things, bad things will fill your brain. It you think about good things, good things will fill your head. If you choose to worry, your brain will be filled with worry, and it may even result in depression. The admonition is to find something good to think about, and then think about it.

Happy people think happy thoughts. Sad people think sad thoughts. The world is full to the brim of bad things about which you can think nonstop. ARE YOU GETTING THIS? What you think about is a choice that you ultimately make.

Now then, let's apply that to evangelism. If you think about evangelism, it will lead you to become evangelistic. Since we get to choose what to think about, we surely must decide what's important enough to spend time considering. It stands to reason that thinking about ETERNAL matters would carry more weight than temporal matters, as long as the eternal matters are things that you can affect. You can affect who goes to heaven, but you cannot change what heaven is like. Paul again tells us to think eternally in Colossians 3:2:

> *"Set your affection on things above, not on things on the earth."*

WHAT SHOULD I THINK ABOUT?

<u>Think about people</u>. When you meet someone, what do you think about them? Do you wonder if they are religious? Do you think about their past life? Do you consider their journey in life? Do you imagine them as prosperous? Do you think about their status, education, job, parents, ethnicity, or cultural heritage? Perhaps you could wonder if they are spiritually connected with God through Jesus. It would require a paradigm shift to get to that point, but it could prove invaluable, especially in the area of personal evangelism. It's a start.

<u>Think about your purpose in life</u>. Such a thought is not uncommon. People generally would like to think that they have a higher purpose. For a follower of Jesus, finding your purpose is fairly easy. Simply by following the teachings and commands of Jesus, we have some clear marching orders. Every evangelical knows and may even quote the idea of the "Great Commission." In the most simple way, embracing that mind-set can have eternal implications. Try to measure earning enough money to buy a cabin in the mountains with leading a young man to Jesus, resulting in his eternal life. The cabin may be nice, comfortable

and provide you with hours, days, even years of pleasure. The young man's soul, according to Jesus, is more valuable than all of that, plus all the world. Mark 8:

> "^{36} For what shall it profit a man, if he shall gain the whole world, and lose his own soul?"

Every person reading this knows Jesus said it, but you will have to ask Him to help you comprehend it.

As a young man in 1973, I yielded myself to God to fulfill His purpose through Jesus. I purposed to spend my life sharing the message of Jesus to as many people as God would allow. In my case, that decision caused me to leave secular work and spend the rest of my days and years focused on spreading the message of John 3:

> "^{16} For God so loved the world that He gave His only begotten Son, that whoever believes in Him should not perish but have everlasting life."

It has been my great privilege to lead several thousand people to Jesus over the last 40 years. In many cases, I have been honored to see the results of the spiritual changes that God has made in the lives of these converts. Many of them have led others to Jesus, and some have even become pastors and missionaries. The ripple effect has been very satisfying in my life, and I can say that I have succeeded in finding and living my purpose.

I believe I can say with the Apostle Paul in II Timothy 4:

> "^{7} I have fought the good fight, I have finished the race, I have kept the faith."

This is not a brag, only an illustration. It is possible to live a fulfilled life.

Think about what God wants. Years ago, I went golfing without a partner. I never did that and haven't done it since because part of the pleasure of golf is to enjoy the fellowship of others. This time, however, I went alone. I was paired with another guy who also arrived alone. As we walked down the first fairway, we began to talk. We asked each other what we did for a living and other small talk. I told the fellow that I was a minister. He immediately replied, "I believe in God." I thought that the quick reply was rather interesting. Was it supposed to end the conversation about spiritual things? I didn't know. From nowhere (ha) I heard myself say, "What do you think He wants?" I hadn't actually given the question much thought. He replied that he didn't know. I gave a quick reply about his eternal destiny, and before we ended the round, he accepted Jesus as his Savior.

That's a thought provoking question to me still to this day, and I've often considered it. Actually, it might be good to ask God every day: "What do You want me to do today? Where do You want me to go?" I recently had a minor surgical procedure, and was soon discharged. A complication sent me back to the hospital where I spent several unpleasant days feeling miserable. I wasn't interested in anyone or anything. As I began to feel better, I became concerned for a man in the next bed. He kept mentioning death, and seemed anxious. I engaged him and was pleased to lead him to Jesus. I didn't want to be in the hospital, but apparently God wanted me there for His divine appointment. Who knew?

You might say, "I can't remember to ask God every day what He wants." EXACTLY! It takes being very intentional to reach a point where you naturally have your spiritual antennae raised.

Listen to what people are saying. Sooner or later people will tell you what's on their mind or heart. Jesus said in Matt. 12:34:

"Out of the abundance of the heart the mouth speaks."

If you keep your spiritual antennae up, you will hear a call for help. People complain a lot. Sometimes they complain about what they perceive they need but don't have. Everyone wants to be at peace. A complaint quite often is an appeal for peace. If you're paying attention, you will easily hear it. Sometimes people express a need that they don't even recognize. During my years in Portugal, a seeker group host told me that he wanted to invite a neighboring business owner to his group. He thought that because the owner was a Scientologist, he probably wouldn't want to come. I don't consider a Scientologist a lost cause, but a seeker. His attempts to connect with God through various religions had failed, and he was trying Scientology to try to make some sense out of it all. It sounds different when you say it like that.

A person is having trouble with his teenage sons. Does that qualify as a cry for spiritual help? It was for my father. He had three teenage boys, and life was very difficult. We were always doing what boys do--stretching him. His heart was in turmoil even though it never occurred to any of us. When offered the opportunity to invite God into his life, he jumped. I owe my spiritual walk to that critical juncture in his life.

I HAVE CANCER! Does that sound like "I need Jesus" to you? It did to me. When I was a corporate chaplain, an employee named Charles said that to me one night. I spent a few minutes trying to console him, then heard myself say, "Cancer is over my pay grade. I don't know what God might have in mind, but I would be glad to ask Him for help. But before I do, let's get God in you, then we can go to Him together and both ask Him for help. What do you say?" Charles thought that it was a good idea to take his need to the highest level and ask for help. Within just a few minutes, Charles had accepted Jesus as his Savior.

Together we prayed for God to bless his life. Within two weeks, Charles told me that his doctor told him that he didn't think that he had cancer. Did God intervene? You can decide. The point is that I was listening for spiritual needs. They are everywhere.

Practice. Nothing is ever easy the first time you try it. Children must learn to crawl, stand, walk, and finally run. When my son was small, he tried t-ball and was disappointed that he was no good at it. The first time that he tried to hit the ball from the tee, he failed. He said that he was no good at baseball. I couldn't convince him that no one was good at baseball the first time they tried. He never pursued it.

I remember the first time I heard someone share their faith. I told myself that I should become good at that. I worked and worked to get it down to where I was comfortable sharing the Gospel. It managed to get into my heart so deeply that I deemed it important enough to become competent at it. It was a decision I made, and then stayed at it until I mastered the art.

How do you get to Carnegie Hall? Practice, practice, practice.

Testify Intentionally

"God's plan for enlarging His kingdom is so simple--one person telling another about the Savior. Yet we're busy and full of excuses. Just remember, someone's eternal destiny is at stake. The joy you'll have when you meet that person in heaven will far exceed any discomfort you felt in sharing the gospel."
-- Charles Stanley

In an effort to share their faith, many people talk about church. They might invite someone to church. Perhaps there is a special musical or event, and they feel that their friends might actually come. In today's American culture, many people feel that attending church is just not for them. In fact, surveys have been made that indicate many Americans are fed up with church as well as organized religion. Unfortunately, most people equate God with religion. In an attempt not to be religious, they avoid or ignore all attempts to introduce them to God.

Any believer who desires to share his faith should learn to share HIS own faith. Talking about church does not convey a personal experience or a personal message. Asking someone to an event, though certainly not wrong, is not sharing your faith. Part of our responsibility as believers is to be capable of effectively sharing Jesus with a lost world. I Peter 3:15:

> *"But sanctify the Lord God in your hearts: and be ready always to give an answer to every man that asks you a reason of the **hope** that is in you with meekness and fear."*

A good "testimony" should include three aspects: 1) what my life was like before Jesus, 2) what actually happened to me (this should explain your encounter with Jesus), 3) what has my life been like since. This testimony should not take over 5 minutes to share. People simply will not tolerate a long, drawn-out story. They will zone out. You must learn to share your story briefly.

What my life was like before. Give some thought to this. What was your life like before you met Jesus? Were you searching for something? Was there a life event that caused you to reach out? Was there some pain that caused you to seek relief? Were you spiritually confused? Maybe you felt emptiness. Perhaps someone in your life shared the Gospel with you, and you saw the need. Was there some kind of loss? This is how it usually happens. God designed life so we would need Him sooner or later.

If you had a need, be sure that someone else has felt the same need. As you share the first part of your testimony, you may touch a nerve within someone else's heart. This is the purpose of sharing your testimony.

The Apostle Paul used his testimony often. *What was his life like before?* Acts 26:

> "**4** *My manner of life from my youth, which was at the first among mine own nation at Jerusalem, know all the Jews;* **5** *Which knew me from the beginning, if they would testify, that after the most strait sect of our religion I lived a Pharisee.* **6** *And now I stand and am judged for the hope of the promise made of God, unto our fathers:* **7** *Unto which promise our twelve tribes, instantly serving God day and night, hope to come. For which hope's sake, King Agrippa, I am accused of the Jews.* **8** *Why should it be thought a thing incredible with you, that God should raise the dead?* **9** *I verily thought with myself, that I ought to do many things contrary to the name of Jesus of Nazareth.* **10** *Which thing I also did in Jerusalem: and many of the saints did I shut up in prison, having received authority*

> *from the chief priests; and when they were put to death, I gave my voice against them. ¹¹ And I punished them oft in every synagogue, and compelled them to blaspheme; and being exceedingly mad against them, I persecuted them even unto strange cities. ¹² Whereupon as I went to Damascus with authority and commission from the chief priests."*

He is saying that he was clearly bound up in his religion and thought that he was defending it by persecuting believers. It seems that he was a terrorist.

<u>What actually happened to me.</u> Here you should describe the spiritual encounter that you had with Jesus. This is when you were truly born again. How many times have I heard people talk about conversion and the narrative never mentioned Jesus. Too often people speak about going to church. They may even tell about how they felt while going to this spiritual place. It may be significantly different from anything that they have ever experienced. I can't help wondering how many people have been introduced to a "more spiritual way" but have never been born again.

Once again, Paul spoke of **his** encounter with Jesus in Acts 26:

> *"¹³ At midday, O King, I saw in the way a light from heaven, above the brightness of the sun, shining round about me and them which journeyed with me. ¹⁴ And when we were all fallen to the earth, I heard a voice speaking unto me, and saying in the Hebrew tongue, Saul, Saul, why are you persecuting me? It is hard for thee to kick against the pricks. ¹⁵ And I said, Who are you, Lord? And he said, I am Jesus whom you are persecuting."*

Now that's an encounter with Jesus. His wasn't the same as mine which wasn't the same as yours, but they were all encounters, nevertheless.

Were you in church when it happened? Then say it. Were you in your car? Tell about it. Did someone help you? Give those details, briefly. But above all, your experience must include Jesus.

<u>*What has my life been like since?*</u> How did the experience change you? Did you find meaning in your life? Did you find peace? Was a burden lifted from your shoulders? Did you feel something? Did you feel nothing? Did it take some time to realize that God had changed your heart? Has your life gone in a different direction?

Everyone is different. No two stories are exactly the same, but telling your story will help people know and understand that God is in the saving and changing business. Here is what Paul said about his life since his conversion. God sent him to the Gentile nations. Acts 26:

> "*[16] But rise, and stand upon thy feet: for I have appeared unto thee for this purpose, to make thee a minister and a witness both of these things which thou hast seen, and of those things in the which I will appear unto thee; [17] Delivering thee from the people, and from the Gentiles, unto whom now I send thee, [18] To open their eyes, and to turn them from darkness to light, and from the power of Satan unto God, that they may receive forgiveness of sins, and inheritance among them which are sanctified by faith that is in me. [19] Whereupon, O King Agrippa, I was not disobedient unto the heavenly vision: [20] But shewed first unto them of Damascus, and at Jerusalem, and throughout all the coasts of Judaea, and then to the*

Gentiles, that they should repent and turn to God, and do works meet for repentance."

Clearly, Paul's life had changed. He stopped persecuting believers and joined their effort. He joined the cause of Jesus. He traveled around the eastern world sharing the gospel message with everyone, everywhere he went. WOW! God is in the saving and changing business.

IN MY CASE, I was invited to church, as a young man, by an attractive girl. My motivation was not spiritual. While there, I heard a Biblical presentation (sermon) about my need for Jesus as my Savior. At the end of the service, I responded by indicating that I wanted to learn more. It sounded like something I needed in my life, and it made sense to me. Someone led me through the Scripture and explained to me how it all works. He showed me that I was a sinner (with which I had no argument). He showed me that the penalty for sin was death, death in hell. He then showed me that Jesus died for my sin, died in my place. Finally, he showed me that if I would accept Him as my savior, I would be spiritually born again. I thought, why not? I couldn't think of any reason to reject the idea. If it were not true, then nothing would actually happen. That day, I opened my heart to Jesus and asked Him to be my Savior. He complied. He entered my life and changed me forever. Since that day, I have told my story several thousand times in hundreds of places to thousands of people, in over a dozen countries. My life now has purpose and is of eternal worth.

As you tell your story, people may be able to relate to you and be drawn to Jesus to meet their own personal needs.

Spend some time and intentionally write your testimony. It is a most invaluable tool for effectively spreading the message. It worked fabulously for Paul. It will work for you.

Teach Intentionally

"The mediocre teacher tells. The good teacher explains. The superior teacher demonstrates. The great teacher inspires."
-- William Ward

"Plant a word in the mind, and you will reap an act. Plant the act and you will reap a habit. Plant a habit and you will reap a character. Plant a character and you will reap a nature. Plant a nature and you will reap a destiny."
-- Unknown

If, in fact, the western Church has lost its way in the area of personal evangelism, the fault must lie with the message being taught by its leaders, its teachers. It seems, as a result of our itching ears, that we embraced the very teachers who have failed to lead us to fulfill the Great Commission. We were warned about such feckless leaders by Paul to Timothy II Timothy 4:1

> *"I charge thee therefore before God, and the Lord Jesus Christ, who shall judge the quick and the dead at his appearing and his kingdom; [2] Preach the word; be instant in season, out of season; reprove, rebuke, exhort with all long suffering and doctrine. [3] For the time will come when they will not endure sound doctrine; but after their own lusts shall they heap to themselves teachers, having itching ears; [4] And they shall turn away their ears from the truth, and shall be turned unto fables."*

Today, we embrace the preacher who makes us feel the best, not the one who challenges us the most. Our success is measured by the size of our buildings, not how many missionaries we send. Our preachers seem to be constantly politicking for more acclaim or a higher office. Believers are drawn to the latest "thing" whether it is a new study guide, a famous preacher's annotated Bible, the TV ratings of our favorite speaker, which female evangelist can draw the largest crowd, or how many satellite churches our group can oversee. I am fascinated that a very public preacher will come to our town, rent the sports' stadium and draw thousands of people. They will preach the same message they preached on TV, still not challenging for world evangelism, sell thousands of feel-good books, and then leave town with every person who attended never reaching out to others as a result of the message. But it made them feel good and they all said, "What a wonderful message."

I know of a nearby church that does not call its congregation 'members' but, instead, calls them 'missionaries'. What a great idea! I know of another church that requires its members to have passports so that they can go on mission trips. How novel! If American churches would give as much weight to evangelism as the Bible does, we would change the world.

One of my favorite Scriptures that I use to validate my life and ministry is Eph. 4:11-16. Just before the quote is a statement telling that Jesus gave "gifts" to men, believers, followers of Jesus. The gifts given are PEOPLE through whom He will accomplish His purpose. The specific gifts are:

> "*11 And He Himself gave some to be apostles, some prophets, some evangelists, and some pastors and teachers.*"

It surely seems that God never intended for anyone to go down the spiritual path alone. God puts people in your life who can help you put your life and priorities right. These people are

> "*12 for the equipping of the saints for the work of ministry, for the edifying of the body of Christ.*"

The matters in focus are "working the ministry" which includes "the edifying of the Body of Christ."

We know that part of the "work of the ministry" is the Great Commission. We have been given the "ministry of reconciliation" (II Cor. 5:18), reconciling a lost world to Jesus. The length of the single sentence from Ephesians 4 is quite remarkable to me. It starts with verse 11 (above) and continues through verse 16:

> "*^{13} till we all come to the unity of the faith and of the knowledge of the Son of God, to a perfect man, to the measure of the stature of the fullness of Christ; ^{14} that we should no longer be children, tossed to and fro and carried about with every wind of doctrine, by the trickery of men, in the cunning craftiness of deceitful plotting, ^{15} but, speaking the truth in love, may grow up in all things into Him who is the head—Christ—^{16} from whom the whole body, joined and knit together by what every joint supplies, according to the effective working by which every part does its share, causes growth of the body for the edifying of itself in love.*"

Imagine the effect of such a spiritual mechanism, the Church. The world would be quite different if our "mentors" led us to such spiritual heights. We would be people who evangelize, are united in our efforts, live holy lives, steadfast in doctrine, share truth lovingly, become spiritually mature, find our place in the Body of Christ, are involved, are growing the body and who are bathed in love. It sounds unstoppable to me.

If a preacher has the Great Commission as a guide to ministry, it is surprising how many Scriptures will highlight evangelism. Can you overdo it? That is the kind of question that causes us to water down the Church's purpose. All that it takes is for the Great

Commission to become the filter through which the preacher/teacher prepares his messages.

The following section contains lesson outlines from certain passages of Scripture that can be used to challenge people to personal evangelism. The goal is to turn your class/church/group evangelistic.

Make it Evangelistic

This is not a test! For over 40 years, this minister has been practicing and teaching personal evangelism. Several thousand people have accepted Jesus as a result. Over the years, it has been my practice and privilege to lead three churches into the arena of evangelism, creating a climate for constant involvement for the Kingdom. The material and methods found in this packet have been tried and proven over four decades of practice.

Contained in this packet are 12 Bible lessons to be taught over a three-month period. Each lesson will challenge the hearer to be involved in personal evangelism and demonstrate the amount of weight that Scripture places on the matter.

Purpose

The purpose of this packet is to help each student learn the Great Commission and learn the value of fulfilling it. Enough work should be done until each student is comfortable enough with their own testimony and technique that they are not afraid to approach people in their own circle.

Philosophy

The first challenge to accomplishing the stated purpose is to get everyone THINKING about personal evangelism. By a simple act of handing the members a tract and asking them to give it to someone this week, it will burn a hole in their pockets and in their minds. Even if they don't hand it out, they will at least think about it. Facebook is a great tool for providing daily reminders for each homework assignment. Of course, some people in the class will catch on to the ideas, but certainly everyone won't. If just a couple of people catch fire, the others will constantly watch them burn. Their fire will get everyone thinking about personal evangelism.

Training must be provided to help each person at least feel competent to win someone to Jesus. This will be done on a weekly schedule. Some will learn quickly and lead the charge.

Weekly Dialogue

Engage a leadership team within the department.

I. Testimonials – 10 minutes

   The purpose of this exercise is to have people voice their experiences. This will challenge others.

II. Instruction – 10 minutes

   Subjects include: presentation, venue, asking for a decision, bridge statements, being intentional, sharing philosophy, testimony, practicing, and challenges.

III. Applicable Bible Lesson – 30 minutes - See lesson outlines

IV. Prayer for lost people – 5 minutes - See prayer sheet

V. Homework - See Homework topics

Everything Rises and Falls on Leadership

The practical as well as philosophical purpose of developing a class structure has several parts:

1. Creating an inner circle of responsibility distributes responsibility for operating a successful class. Having an inner circle also creates a sense of ownership for certain class members. They will be the most dependable members of the class.

2. Part of the function of this team is to constantly expand itself, drawing more people into the inner circle, thus creating more dependable members.

3. By delegating authority for class function, the burden is spread over the group so that it does not become too burdensome for just one or two people. It is quite possible to "burn out" people who serve by overtaxing them in their Christian service.

4. A statement of purpose should drive the actions of this inner circle. Clear direction is important to create a central theme for the class. Every activity of the class should be filtered through the purpose to ensure that the class does not lose vision.

5. This group functions as a monitoring force to keep things moving forward. People do what you inspect, not what you expect. In a congenial way, these leaders provide constant reminders to the class of its duties.

6. Two rules for class growth exist, namely: Keep what you've got. Get some more. Those things that are required to "keep what you've got": challenge, personal growth, spiritual growth, Bible knowledge, Christian service, and a sense of community will help to keep what you've got. Developing a broad spectrum of ways to reach outside of the group will facilitate "getting some more."

This spectrum of outreach should be graded to include every member to constantly stretch them to new levels of service.

Offices for the Leadership Team

Director

This person should be totally invested in the success of the class. With the above information in mind, he should lead the class to fulfill the mission statement. New ideas should be filtered through the mission statement to ensure compatibility. The Director should constantly monitor the functions of each separate department team. Constant supervision is the way of insuring against diminished activity in each group. Every action of these groups should be approved by the Director. The Director MUST be a self-starter who does not need supervising.

Outreach Leader

By definition, the Outreach Leader should provide venues for outreach that can be performed by any class member. Some people can go on mission trips to other countries. Some people can invite to a seeker group. Some will like to feed homeless. Some can hand out a tract. Some can share their faith. Some will actually lead people to Jesus. Some people will be good at befriending class prospects or fringe members. Some should engage with the church outreach office to follow-up on new people to the church. Each outreach venue should agree in principle with the mission statement. Weekly reports or encouragement should be given to the class to ensure constant exposure to outreach.

In-reach Leader

Within the scope of "keep what you've got" this person should constantly seek out issues within families that would hinder them from being involved within the class. This person can delegate to class members the responsibility of reaching within the class to demonstrate care for the members of the class. It would be awesome if each member of the class met with every other member of the class for a time of fellowship and to create a new level of intimacy as they learn more about each other. COMMUNITY is one thing that people desire and require. The more "community", the more satisfying the class will be.

Refreshments Leader

Refreshments have a twofold purpose. The obvious is to provide refreshments within the class during class time as well as for special events. The second purpose is to give class members responsibility within the class. The more people who have responsibility, the more ownership members have for their class.

Events Leader

From time to time, the class should have events, in keeping with the mission statement, that help foster relationships within the group. These events can also be intentionally planned to include outsiders, fringe members, and new prospects to the church.

Instructions

Each week some instructions should be given to help along the process. Some of these instructions can be found printed in the book *Charging Hell with a Squirt Gun*. Hand out the book in the first class. It will be a good resource going forward. Some will read it, some won't. At some point they still may. The items listed below are designed to equip the saints for the work of the ministry.

Romans Road map. Teach each member how to map their Bible with the Romans Road. It won't take much class time to discuss this because it is in the book.

Testimony. Each member should learn how to develop their own testimony. Several rules should be followed. It should be no more than five minutes. Any longer and it gets boring. It should contain three elements: (1) what was my life before (2) what happened to me [this should include the name Jesus] (3) what has my life been like since. This testimony should be written. It is harder than it sounds. It should contain no religious language, language that needs explaining.

Using tracts. When and how to use a tract. Probably when nothing else can be done for constraint of time (waitresses, etc.).

Oikos - your circle. This idea should be taught with the Oikos PowerPoint lesson. We are all connected to someone who needs Jesus.

Intentionality. This lesson will help students learn to keep their antennae up.

Bridge statements. There is a chapter in the book about this. A bridge statement is one that transitions from life to the Gospel without being clumsy.

Presentation. If a dying man came to you and asked how to connect with God, what would you tell him? You should be comfortable; tell him.

Asking for a decision. There is a difference between sharing your faith and asking for a decision. It is the difference between chumming and fishing. One catches fish and the other doesn't.

Practice. Are you good at what you do? How did you get that way? This skill is worth perfecting.

Venue. Where will you share the Gospel? You must decide on a venue that you can perfect; perhaps in the street with the homeless, perhaps in the prison with prisoners, perhaps in a seeker group, perhaps door to door, perhaps with church visitors, perhaps with friends.

Bring them. Once a person becomes a believer, how will you help them going forward? Perhaps it would be helpful to bring them to church or class.

Cross cultures. Cultures do not necessarily mean ethnic cultures. It could mean reaching people of other age groups. Differences certainly exist.

Lessons

See the lesson handout sheets. The ones with **THIS PRINT** are for the teacher. **THIS PRINT** is a starter statement.

Homework

Write it. Write your testimony. Give your testimony to someone.

Watch a video. www.seekerministry.com → instructions → seeker instruction video

Read the book. Read *Charging Hell with a Squirt Gun*.

Mark your Bible. Use the above book and mark your Bible for the Romans Road.

Start praying. Begin to pray for lost people, not sick people.

Listen for pain. During daily conversations listen for peoples' complaints. They are many. We have the answer.

Spiritual language. Begin to use language that talks about God, blessings, and spiritual things.

Talk together. Find someone to listen to your testimony.

Hand out a tract. Find a person who could use some help. What would you say?

Start a group. By using the invitation and the script, invite people to a group. "Hey Joe, you may know that I am on a bit of a spiritual journey. This man (flyer) has agreed to help me along the way and said that I could invite some others also. You are welcome to come; we are meeting at ……..''

Get a decision. What would you say to ask a person to accept Jesus? It's in the book.

Class Mission Statement

Once the idea of personal evangelism gets into the heads of the students, ask them to help develop a mission statement for the class. From that day forward, everything done in the class including in-reach, outreach, and events should be measured against the mission statement for compatibility.

Nothing But Leaves – Matthew 21

It has always been the plan of God to provide redemption to all the world, not just be the God of the Jews.

I. Why is Jesus picking on this poor tree? v. 18-20

II. Jesus explains His actions. Who do the players in this drama represent? v. 33

III. Another set of players. What is this fruit? v. 34

IV. Match other Scripture with this mistreatment. v. 35-36

V. Of course you know Who the Son is. v. 37-39

VI. This is a Jewish trick to get the people to condemn themselves. v. 40

VII. They condemned their own actions. v. 41

VIII. Jesus uses prophecy to identify Himself. Also used by Peter. Acts 4:11 v. 42

IX. Their future would be like the fig tree in v. 19, cursed. v. 43

X. Their only hope, offered. v. 44

XI. Rejected. v. 45-46

Nothing But Leaves – Matthew 21

It has always been the plan of God to provide redemption to all the world, not just be the God of the Jews. **GENESIS 12:1-4, PSALM 67.**

I. Why is Jesus picking on this poor tree? v. 18-20

THE FIG TREE REPRESENTS THE NATION OF ISRAEL. MATTHEW 24:32 THIS ACTION IS PROPHETIC.

II. Jesus explains His actions. Who do the players in this drama represent? v. 33

HOUSEHOLDER, GOD; VINEYARD, THE WORLD; HUSBANDMEN, ISRAEL; COUNTRY, HEAVEN.

III. Another set of players. What is this fruit? v. 34

SERVANTS = PROPHETS. FRUIT = CONVERTS.

IV. Match other Scripture with this mistreatment? v. 35-36

MATTHEW 23:37, HEBREWS 11:36-39.

V. Of course you know Who the Son is. v. 37-39

HERE, JESUS IS PREDICTING HIS OWN DEATH.

VI. This is a Jewish trick to get the people to condemn themselves. v. 40

NATHAN DID THIS TO DAVID.

VII. They condemned their own actions.   v. 41

OTHER, GENTILE NATIONS. THEIR SEASON, NOW. MAKE NO MISTAKE, JESUS EXPECTS FRUIT, CONVERTS.

VIII. Jesus uses prophecy to identify Himself. Also used by Peter. Acts 4:11   v. 42

PROPHECY IS THE VALIDATING PART OF SCRIPTURE. LUKE 24:27, ACTS 2:16, 25, 30.

IX. There future would be like the fig tree in v. 19, cursed. v. 43

MATTHEW. 24:1-2

X. Their only hope, offered.   v. 44

THIS IS THE ONLY HOPE OF EVERY MAN. JOHN 3:16

XI. Rejected.   v. 45-46

EVERYONE CHOOSES.

The Good Samaritan – Luke 10:25-37

Introduction: The accounts recorded in the Bible were selected for very distinct purposes. Throughout the Gospels nothing is incidental. The account of the Good Samaritan should be filtered through the Great Commission. It is not just "a day in the life" of Jesus. See if you can figure out the main message of the story.

I. Who is this lawyer? What's he all about? v. 25

II. Why did Jesus give this answer? v. 26-28

III. What was in the lawyer's heart? The answer is in the answer. v. 29

IV. Notice the details Jesus gives to the lawyer. Dig deep.

v. 30-32

V. Why did Jesus inject a Samaritan into this story? (Hint: the lawyer was Jewish.) v. 33

VI. What does this mean at the spiritual level? v. 34

VII. Can you see the eschatology in this verse? v. 35

VIII. A Jewish trick?   v. 36

IX. The punch line. What is the failure of the lawyer?   v. 37

Instruction: Using tracts – why, how.

Homework: Read the book.

The Good Samaritan – Luke 10:25-37

Introduction: The accounts recorded in the Bible were selected for very distinct purposes. Throughout the Gospels nothing is incidental. The account of the Good Samaritan should be filtered through the Great Commission. It is not just "a day in the life" of Jesus. See if you can figure out the main message of the story.

NOTES IN THIS FONT ARE STARTER NOTES FOR THE TEACHER.

I. Who is this lawyer? What's he all about?   v. 25

HE WAS: JEWISH, FULL OF LAW BUT BEARING NO FRUIT, DISHONEST, HYPOCRITICAL. HONEST QUESTIONS ARE GOOD; THIS ONE WAS NOT.

II. Why did Jesus give this answer? v. 26-28

JESUS BEGAN TO EXPOSE HIS HEART. THIS IS CERTAINLY NOT THE ANSWER FOR SALVATION.

III. What was in the lawyer's heart? The answer is in the answer. v. 29

SELF-JUSTIFICATION IS A VERY COMMON MALADY. WHAT IS LOVE ANYWAY? HOW IS IT DISPLAYED?

IV. Notice the details Jesus gives to the lawyer. Dig deep.

v. 30-32

THE PLAYERS IN THIS STORY MEAN SOMETHING. THE NAKED MAN WAS UNDISTINGUISHABLE BECAUSE OF HIS LACK OF STATUS CLOTHING. THE LAWYER WOULD NOT

EVEN KNOW IF HE SHOULD HELP HIM FOR LACK OF INFORMATION. WHAT IS HALF DEAD? IN THIS CONTEXT IT SEEMS TO BE SPIRITUAL DEATH. THE PRIEST REPRESENTED RELIGION WHICH IS UNABLE TO HELP A PERSON SPIRITUALLY DEAD. THE LEVITE WAS A KEEPER OF THE LAW WHICH IS LIKEWISE IMPOTENT.

V. Why did Jesus inject a Samaritan into this story? (Hint: the lawyer was Jewish.) v. 33

THE SAMARITAN WOULD REPRESENT A CROSS-CULTURAL EXPERIENCE, WHICH THE LAWYER WOULD DISDAIN.

VI. What does this mean at the spiritual level? v. 34

THE SAMARITAN (JOHN 4, THE JEWS HAVE NO DEALINGS WITH THE SAMARITANS) HAD COMPASSION; THE LAWYER DID NOT. THE LAWYER HAD THE REQUIREMENT TO SHARE HIS FAITH BUT THE SAMARITAN ACTUALLY DID IT. OIL (HOLY SPIRIT) AND WINE (JOY) MAY INDICATE SALVATION. FOR SURE THE JEWS WERE REQUIRED TO EVANGELIZE THE WORLD.

ONCE "SAVED" THE SAMARITAN WENT A STEP FURTHER: HE BROUGHT HIM TO THE INN AND TOOK CARE OF HIM. (THIS IS WHERE THE MOST WORK COMES IN.) WHAT IS THE INN? PERHAPS IT IS THE CHURCH.

VII. Can you see the eschatology in this verse? v. 35

MONEY IS INVOLVED IN THIS PROCESS. WHO IS THE HOST? PERHAPS IT IS A DISCIPLE FOR FURTHER HELP

(DISCIPLESHIP, EPHESIANS 4:10-11). IS JESUS COMING AGAIN? THE EFFORT WILL BE REWARDED.

VIII. A Jewish trick? v. 36

THIS IS A SOCRATIC METHOD OF HELPING THE QUESTIONER ANSWER HIS OWN QUESTION. REMEMBER NATHAN TO DAVID?

IX. The punch line. What is the failure of the lawyer? v. 37

THE LAWYER'S PREJUDICE WOULD NOT EVEN ALLOW HIM TO SAY THE WORD SAMARITAN. TWO SUBJECTS ANSWERED IN ONE: WHAT IS LOVE AND WHAT IS MY RESPONSIBILITY? TO SPREAD THE WAY TO GOD TO THE LOST WORLD.

The Great Commission - Matthew 28:19-20

(The Christian's Career)

When we get to heaven we will realize that this is the highest priority on earth, spreading the message of God and convincing others to accept it. This will prove to be of greater significance than your job, your hobbies, your lawn, your toys and even your family. This is the Christian's career.

I. Go

> The Bible says, "Go"; church buildings say, "Come".
>
> Where to go? John 1:41, family. Mark 5:19, friends. Acts 5:45, every house. Acts 1:8, the world.

II. Teach

> Not religion.
>
> About Jesus. Matthew 11:28-30, John 1:7-9, John 6:45, John 14:6

III. Baptize

> Signal the decision. Matthew 10:32

IV. Teach

> Ephesians 4:12, II Corinthians 5:18-20

V. This command should govern:

> Where you: live, work, go to school, play, spend your spare time.
>
> How you: Live your life, choose a mate, select a job, invest your money.

What you do with: Bible study, prayer, sermons you hear, friends you choose, giving.

VI. This is your career

VII. I am with you

Instructions: Develop a useful testimony.

Homework: Watch a video this week.

<u>www.seekerministry.com</u> → instructions → seeker outline hardcopy → seeker instruction video

The Great Commission - Matthew 28:19-20

(The Christian's Career)

When we get to heaven we will realize that this is the highest priority on earth, spreading the message of God and convincing others to accept it. This will prove to be of greater significance that your job, your hobbies, your lawn, your toys, and even your family. This is the Christian's career.

NOTES IN THIS FONT ARE INITIATING THOUGHTS ABOUT EACH ITEM.

I. Go

The Bible says, "Go"; church buildings say, "Come".

A BALANCE CAN BE ACHIEVED, BUT WESTERN EUROPE IS FULL OF EMPTY CHURCHES. CHINA, WHERE REVIVAL HAS STARTED, HAS NONE.

Where to go? John 1:41, family. Mark 5:19, friends. Acts 5:45, every house. Acts 1:8, the world.

JOHN 1 - FAMILY. RELATIONAL EVANGELISM YIELDS MORE SOLID BELIEVERS VIA AUTOMATIC DISCIPLESHIP.

    MARK 5 - FRIENDS. SAME.

    ACTS 5 - COMMUNITY. WE ARE ALL SERIOUSLY CONNECTED.

    ACTS 1 - UTTERMOST WORLD. GO, BUT AT LEAST SEND. ROMANS 10:14-17

II. Teach

Not religion.

RELIGION CLASSES ARE THE MOST COMMON CLASSES IN CHRISTIANITY.

About Jesus. Matthew 11:28-30, John 1:7-9, John 6:45, John 14:6

MATTHEW - REST FOR YOUR SOUL IN JESUS.

JOHN 1 - HE IS THE LIGHT TO EVERY MAN.

JOHN 6 - JESUS IS GOD IN THE FLESH.

JOHN 14 - THE WAY, THE TRUTH, AND THE LIFE.

III. Baptize

Signal the decision. Matthew 10:32

BAPTISM IS NOT THE DECISION BUT SIGNALS THE DECISION.

MATTHEW - PUBLIC CONFESSION PLEASES THE FATHER. PLEASING THE FATHER IS A GOOD PRACTICE.

IV. Teach

Ephesians 4:12, II Corinthians 5:18-20

EPHESIANS - PERFECT THE SAINTS FOR THE WORK OF THE MINISTRY.

II CORINTHIANS - THE MINISTRY IS ONE OF RECONCILIATION: THE LOST WORLD TO GOD.

V. This command should govern:

Where you: live, work, go to school, play, spend your spare time.

WORK SHOULD NOT CONSUME YOUR LIFE. IT SHOULD BE A MEANS TO AN END, NOT THE END.

SCHOOL SHOULD ALLOW US TO BE SALT AND LIGHT.

PLAY SHOULD NOT BE LIFE'S GOAL; I.E., BOAT, CAMPING, CABIN, FISHING ETC. NONE ARE BAD IN THEMSELVES BUT CAN BECOME ALL IN ALL.

SPARE TIME LETS YOU FUNCTION WITH ETERNITY IN MIND.

How you: live your life, choose a mate, select a job, invest your money.

LIVE INTENTIONALLY. CHOOSE A MATE WITH ETERNAL INTERESTS. SELECT A JOB WHICH PAYS THE BILLS WHILE YOU PERFORM YOUR CAREER. MONEY: LAY NOT UP FOR YOURSELVES TREASURES ON EARTH, BUT IN HEAVEN.

What you do with: Bible study, prayer, sermons you hear, friends you choose, giving.

BIBLE STUDY: TO BE BETTER EQUIPPED TO WIN THE LOST, NOT JUST FILL YOUR HEAD.

PRAYER: FOR ETERNAL THINGS; SOULS.

SERMONS CAN EQUIP YOU WITH GOSPEL IDEAS WHILE YOU EMPOWER YOUR LIFE.

FRIENDS SHOULD BE ALLIES, NOT DISTRACTIONS.

GIVE TO CHANGE HEAVEN, NOT TO CHANGE THE WORLD (SPOTTED OWL). IF I ONLY HAD A DOLLAR TO DONATE, WHERE WOULD I SEND IT? TO ME, TRAINING A NATIONAL WILLING TO INVEST HIS LIFE IN HIS PEOPLE.

VI. This is your career.

VII. I am with you.

THOSE INVOLVED IN THIS ENDEAVOR ENJOY MORE OF THE PRESENCE OF THE HOLY SPIRIT. THEY NEED HIM; MANY OTHERS DO NOT.

Instructions:

Develop a useful testimony.

IT ELIMINATES DEBATE.

I WAS .... THEN ONE DAY .... SINCE THEN.

ADD TO IT A USEFUL QUESTION.

Homework:

Watch a video this week.

www.seekerministry.com --- instructions --- seeker outline hardcopy --- seeker instruction video

The Woman at the Well - John 4

I. Not to create a doctrine.   v. 1-3

II. Why? v. 4

III. What do you know about Samaria? v. 5

IV. Engaged in her world. v. 6-7

V. For the comfort of the woman. v. 8

VI. Crossing cultures. v. 9

VII. Keeping it understandable.   v. 10

VIII. She was drawn in. v. 11-12

IX. Spiritualizing. v. 13-14

X. Of course she didn't get it.   v. 15

XI. Necessary supernatural acknowledgement.   v. 16-19

XII. What was her subject? v. 20

XIII. It's not about mountains.   v. 21-22

XIV. There it is. v. 23-24

XV. She is connecting dots. v. 25

XVI. Guess what! v. 26

XVII. Still steeped in ethnocentricity.   v. 27

XVIII. Come. v. 28-29

XIX. Satisfaction guaranteed. v. 30-34

XX. There is a payoff.   v. 35-38

XXI. What is a testimony? v. 39

Instruction: Bridge statements.

Homework: Read that section of the book.

The Woman at the Well - John 4

I. Not to create a doctrine.   v. 1-3

HAD JESUS DONE THE BAPTIZING, A DOCTRINE WOULD BE CREATED.

II. Why?   v. 4

THIS WAS A DIVINE APPOINTMENT.

III. What do you know about Samaria?   v. 5

DURING THE FIRST DEPORTATION, 721 BC, THE KING OF ASSYRIA SENT IDOLATROUS FOREIGNERS TO THE CITY THAT WOULD INTERMARRY WITH THE JEWS. THIS RESULTED IN THE COMBINING OF RELIGIONS CALLED SYNCRETISM. LATER A JEWISH PRIEST WAS SENT TO THE LAND TO REINSTRUCT THE SAMARITANS BUT THEIR BLOOD LINE WAS SPOILED AND THEY WERE OSTRACIZED BY THE JEWS.

IV. Engaged in her world.   v. 6-7

BRIDGE STATEMENTS SHOULD NOT CREATE OPPOSITION.

V. For the comfort of the woman.   v. 8

SHE WAS NOT PUT ON THE SPOT.

VI. Crossing cultures.   v. 9

THIS CAN EASILY BE DONE WITH CHILDREN, TEENS OR PEOPLE WITH OTHER STANDARDS THAN YOU HAVE.

VII. Keeping it understandable.   v. 10

STILL IN HER WORLD.

VIII. She was drawn in.   v. 11-12

SHE WAS ENGAGED. HER QUESTION WAS PERMISSION TO MOVE FORWARD. I LIKE TO GAIN PERMISSION EVEN IF IT IS A SMALL CONSENT.

IX. Spiritualizing.   v. 13-14

THE SHIFT IS BEING MADE BETWEEN PHYSICAL AND SPIRITUAL. (THREE-LEGGED STOOL.)

X. Of course she didn't get it.   v. 15

PATIENCE.

XI. Necessary supernatural acknowledgement.   v.16-19

NOW IS HAS BECOME SPIRITUAL TO HER. THE SUPERNATURAL IS ACKNOWLEDGED.

XII. What was her subject?   v. 20

SHE THOUGHT IT BEST TO FIGURE OUT THE DIFFERENCE IN RELIGIONS.

XIII. It's not about mountains.   v. 21-22

HE DIDN'T GO THERE.

XIV. There it is.   v. 23-24

WHAT DO THESE WORDS MEAN: WORSHIP, SPIRIT, TRUTH?

XV. She is connecting dots.   v. 25

JESUS PATIENTLY LETS HER FIGURE IT OUT. IT'S GOOD TO BE GOD.

XVI. Guess what!   v. 26

XVII. Still steeped in ethnocentricity.   v. 27

IT WOULD TAKE A SMALL MIRACLE TO GAIN THIS GROUND (PETER DREAMING ABOUT SHEETS AND UNCLEAN ANIMALS).

XVIII. Come.   v. 28-29

SHE BECAME A PART OF THE BRIDE, SHE BELIEVED. THE SPIRIT AND THE BRIDE SAY, "COME." THAT'S YOU.

XIX. Satisfaction guaranteed.   v. 30-34

THIS WILL FINALLY ANSWER YOUR QUESTION, "WHY AM I HERE?" LIVE THE FULFILLED LIFE. HIS WORK IS OUR WORK.

XX. There is a payoff.   v. 35-38

I THESSALONIANS 2:19 - CROWN OF REJOICING, SOULWINNER'S CROWN.

XXI. What is a testimony?   v. 39

SIMPLY TELLING WHAT YOU KNOW ABOUT BEFORE, THE ENCOUNTER, AFTER.

Instruction: Bridge statements.

Homework: Read that section of the book.

Oikos

I. Who was the first person in the Bible said to be filled with the Spirit?

II. Who else was filled with the Spirit? Luke 4:16-21

III. Watch Oikos at work. John 1:35-51

IV. What were they seeking? v. 35-37

V. How to invite. v. 39

VI. Who to invite. v. 40-42

VII. Peter's name changed. v. 42

VIII. What is the connection? v. 43-44

IX. What was the conversation? v. 45

X. Why is it to your advantage? John 16:7

XI. An epiphany. v. 47-49

XII. You haven't seen anything yet. v. 50

XIII. What are the greater works? John 14:12

XIV. Who is the Bride and where is the Spirit? Rev. 22:17

XV. This will blow your mind. v. 51

XVI. What should you do?

Instruction: Invitation.

Joe, as you may know, I am trying to be a follower of Jesus. I just want God to bless my life to the fullest. This guy has agreed to help me with my journey and has agreed to come to my house and teach me what I need to know to get God to bless my life. He said that I could invite others who might want the same thing. You are welcome to come if you like.

Homework: Do it!

Oikos (Use this outline with the PowerPoint)

I. Who was the first person in the Bible said to be filled with the Spirit?

BEZELEL PROBABLY DIDN'T KNOW THAT GOD HAD GIFTED HIM. HIS TASK WAS TO USE HIS SKILL, NOT EXPLAIN IT.

II. Who else was filled with the Spirit? Luke 4:16-21

JESUS DID ALL IN THE POWER OF THE SPIRIT.

III. Watch Oikos at work. John 1:35-51

EACH CIRCLE OF FRIENDS LEADS US TO ANOTHER CIRCLE OF FRIENDS.

IV. What were they seeking? v. 35-37

THEY COULD NOT COME UP WITH A GOOD ANSWER AS TO WHAT THEY WERE SEEKING. EVERYONE IS SEEKING WHETHER THEY KNOW IT OR NOT.

V. How to invite. v. 39

COME AND SEE. IT SEEMS EASY ENOUGH. IF YOU CAN MANAGE A PLACE FOR THEM TO "COME AND SEE", THEY WILL COME. IT NEEDS TO MAKE SENSE.

VI. Who to invite. v. 40-42

YOUR CIRCLE OF INFLUENCE, OIKOS.

VII. Peter's name changed.   v. 42

SEE WHY IN MATTHEW 16:18. BIG STONE VS LITTLE STONE. WHY PETER?

VIII. What is the connection?   v. 43-44

THEY ALL BELONG TO THE SAME COMMUNITY. THIS IS RELATIONAL EVANGELISM.

IX. What was the conversation?   v. 45

ANOTHER "COME AND SEE." HOW HARD IS THIS? IS THIS THREATENING, CONDESCENDING, ANTAGONISTIC?

X. Why is it to your advantage?   John 16:7

THE SPIRIT WILL DESCEND ON ALL BELIEVERS, MULTIPLYING THE FORCES.

XI. An epiphany.   v. 47-49

HE KNOWS YOU. HE KNOWS WHAT YOU NEED TO HEAR AND SEE.

XII. You haven't seen anything yet.   v. 50

ANYONE WHO IS A BELIEVER SEES GREATER THINGS.

XIII. What are the greater works?   John 14:12

IN SHEER VOLUME. HOW MANY WERE "SAVED" AT PENTECOST? HOW MANY WERE IN THE UPPER ROOM? GREATER NUMBERS EXPERIENCED SALVATION WHEN SHARED BY THE BELIEVERS THAN SHARED BY THE SAVIOR.

XIV. Who is the Bride and where is the Spirit?   Revelation 22:17

BELIEVERS ARE THE BRIDE INDWELT BY THE SPIRIT. THE MESSAGE IS SIMPLE, "COME."

XV. This will blow your mind.   v. 51

I SEE THINGS ALL THE TIME THAT BLOW MY MIND. BUT THE BEST IS YET TO COME.

XVI. What should you do?

DUH! KEEP IT SIMPLE.

Instruction: Invitation.

Joe, as you may know, I am trying to be a follower of Jesus. I just want God to bless my life to the fullest. This guy has agreed to help me with my journey and has agreed to come to my house and teach me what I need to know to get God to bless my life. He said that I could invite others who might want the same thing. You are welcome to come if you like.

Homework: Do it!

The Spirit-Filled Church - Acts 2

I. The miraculous event. v. 1-4

II. Don't miss this. v. 5

III. Pay attention. v. 6-13

IV. The purpose of the miracle. v. 14

V. Peter uses the prophets to validate. v. 15-21

    We are in that day now.

VI. More prophecy connecting the dots. v. 22-36

VII. The real question. v. 37

VIII. The answer. v. 38-41

IX. Doctrine, fellowship, probably communion, prayers. v. 42

X. Apostolic gifts.   v. 43   Luke 9:1

XI. Helped each other. v. 44-45

XII. In a man's world, women and children – home groups v. 46

XIII. God is in the saving business. v. 47

XIX. We've come a long way.

Instruction: Venue. Homework: Start a group.

The Spirit-Filled Church - Acts 2

I. The miraculous event.   v. 1-4

THREE MIRACLES. IF YOU CAN'T DO THEM ALL, DON'T DO ANY.

II. Don't miss this.   v. 5

THESE PEOPLE WERE FROM THE DIASPORA. IT WAS A PART OF JEREMIAH 29:11 PLANS. THESE WERE PROBABLY BI-LINGUAL, PERHAPS TRI.

III. Pay attention.   v. 6-13

THREE TIMES WE ARE TOLD THAT THESE WERE KNOWN LANGUAGES.

IV. The purpose of the miracle.   v. 14

DRAW A CROWD. FOCUS THE ATTENTION ON THE DISCIPLES.

V. Peter uses the prophets to validate.   v. 15-21

JESUS DID THIS SAME THING IN LUKE 24. PAUL DID THIS SAME THING IN ACTS 17. PETER DID THIS SAME THING SEVERAL TIMES.

    We are in that day now.

IT DIDN'T USED TO BE THIS SIMPLE; CALLING ON THE NAME OF THE LORD.

VI. More prophecy connecting the dots.   v. 22-36

CONNECT THE DOTS BETWEEN PROPHECY ABOUT THE MESSIAH AND JESUS.

VII. The real question.   v. 37

THE ANSWER TO THIS QUESTION HAS FORMED MANY RELIGIONS.

VIII. The answer.   v. 38-41

REPENT FROM UNBELIEF. BAPTIZE TO SIGNAL THE DECISION. THIS IS NOTHING NEW FOR JEWS.

IX. Doctrine, fellowship, probably communion, prayers.   v. 42

THIS IS THE ANSWER TO JESUS' PRAYER ON JOHN 17: THAT THEY MAY BE ONE.

X. Apostolic gifts.   v. 43   Luke 9:1

I WISH THAT I HAD SUCH GIFTS. I DO HAVE THE SCRIPTURE WHICH THEY DID NOT HAVE.

XI. Helped each other.   v. 44-45

COMMON INTERESTS, COMMON MISSION, COMMON NEEDS.

XII. In a man's world, women and children – home groups. v. 46

ON PENTECOST, IT WAS PROBABLY ALL MEN. IT'S GOOD ENOUGH FOR FAMILY AND FRIENDS.

XIII. God is in the saving business.   v. 47

WAITING FOR US TO OFFER HIM.

XIX. We've come a long way.

ARE WE STILL THE SPIRIT-FILLED CHURCH?

Instruction: Venue.

Homework: Start a group.

The Most Mission-Minded Man in the Bible – Luke 16:19-31

I. Status has nothing to do with salvation.   v. 19-21

    This is not a parable. Parables do not use proper names. One would wonder why this poor beggar was so punished.

II. Oops! He wasn't without God. Where is Abraham's bosom? Why didn't he go to hell?   v. 22

III. More than one torment. Why was he in hell?   v. 23

IV. Hot fire, no water, consciousness.   v. 24

V. Who would have thought that the rich man was not being blessed by God.   v. 25

VI. You can't leave.   v. 26

VII. Not having a party. He did not want company. He became concerned for his family.   v. 27

VIII. Concern for family. Send someone.   v. 28

IX. God's Word has the answer, message, and the warning.   v. 29

X. Zombies don't save. God's only plan is you.   v. 30-31 Psalms 126:6.

XI. This is real. When did this happen?

Instruction: Ask for a decision.

The Most Mission-Minded Man in the Bible – Luke 16:19-31

I. Status has nothing to do with salvation   v. 19-21

    This is not a parable. Parables do not use proper names. One would wonder why this poor beggar was so punished.

PARABLES DO NOT USE PROPER NAMES. THE NAME OF THE RICH MAN IS OMITTED, PERHAPS FOR THE SAKE OF HIS FAMILY. THAT CULTURE MAY HAVE THOUGHT THAT BECAUSE THE BEGGAR WAS POOR THAT GOD WAS NOT IN HIS LIFE.

II. Oops! He wasn't without God. Where is Abraham's bosom? Why didn't he go to hell?   v. 22

WHY WOULD GOD ALLOW ONE OF HIS TO BE POOR? ABRAHAM'S BOSOM WAS ALSO CALLED PARADISE ("TODAY YOU WILL BE WITH ME IN PARADISE"). NO ONE COULD GO TO HEAVEN UNTIL JESUS PAID THE SIN DEBT. THEY WERE IN A HOLDING PLACE WAITING FOR SALVATION (EPHESIANS 4:8-10).

III. More than one torment. Why was he in hell?   v. 23

CONSCIOUSNESS, REGRET, MEMORY, AWARE OF HIS LOT, ENVY.

IV. Hot fire, no water, consciousness   v. 24

THIS IS BAD. THERE IS NO MENTION OF A PARTY OR FELLOWSHIP IN HELL.

V. Who would have thought that the rich man was not being blessed by God.   v. 25

SURELY, IF YOU'RE RICH, YOU ARE BLESSED, RIGHT? ECCLESIASTES 6:1-3.

VI. You can't leave. v. 26

IT IS FOREVER - MARK 9:44, 46, 48.   STILL UNJUDGED - REV. 20:11-15.

VII. Not having a party. He did not want company. He became concerned for his family. v. 27

HELL BECAME A REALITY, NOT JUST A DOCTRINE. IT IS REAL.

VIII. Concern for family. Send someone.   v. 28

ISAIAH 6:8

IX. God's Word has the answer, message, and the warning. v. 29

IF YOU HAD THE ANSWER TO CANCER, WHAT WOULD YOU DO WITH IT? WHAT IF IT WERE HOLISTIC?

X. Zombies don't save. God's only plan is you.   v. 30-31 Psalms 126:6.

THIS IS THE SOULWINNERS' GUARANTEE.

XI. This is real. When did this happen?

THIS PROBABLY HAPPENS EVERY DAY. ISN'T THERE SOMEONE WHO WILL GO TO MY FAMILY? HELL IS FULL OF PEOPLE WITH THE SAME REQUEST.

Instruction: Ask for a decision.

Joseph's Church – Genesis 45

I. Introduction: How he got to Egypt.

II. Joseph reveals his identity.   v. 1-4

III. God sent me here; awesome insight.   v. 5-8

IV. In this place is life.   v. 9-16

V. Sounds like the Great Commission.   v. 17-19

VI. It's not about "stuff" - "Lay not up for yourselves".   v. 20

VII. What provisions are we given?   v. 21-23

VIII. It's easy to get distracted.   v. 24

IX. The message may take convincing.   v. 25-26

X. Here is what it did for me.   v. 27

XI. Some will believe.   v. 28

XII. Is this a heavenly scene?   Genesis 46:29

Joseph's Church – Genesis 45

I. Introduction: How he got to Egypt.

TELL THE STORY OF JOSEPH PRE-AUTHORITY.

II. Joseph reveals his identity.   v. 1-4

They were shocked. This could go badly.

III. God sent me here; awesome insight.   v. 5-8

ALL OF THE TRIAL AND PAIN WAS USED BY GOD, IF NOT DIRECTED BY GOD

IV. In this place is life.   v. 9-16

WHY DO WE DO WHAT WE DO?

V. Sounds like the Great Commission.   v. 17-19

THE KING SHOWED MERCY. SO DOES GOD. BALANCE WITH JUDGMENT.

VI. It's not about "stuff" - "Lay not up for yourselves".   v. 20

OUR WESTERN CULTURE SAYS OTHERWISE.

VII. What provisions are we given?   v. 21-23

BIBLE, HOLY SPIRIT, PRAYER, MONEY. WE WALK THROUGH THIS LIFE, COLLECTING WHAT? "SHOW ME THE FISH."

VIII. It's easy to get distracted   v. 24

WHAT DO WE DO BESIDES GATHER SOULS?

IX. The message may take convincing. v. 25-26

THE MESSAGE OFTEN IS MISUNDERSTOOD.

X. Here is what it did for me.   v. 27

YOUR TESTIMONY HAS GREAT POWER.

XI. V. Some will believe.

CHRIS BRYANT. (OR YOUR OWN CONVERT)

XII. 46:29 Is this a heavenly scene?

SOME GO ON BEFORE YOU. HEB. 12:1-2

Rahab's Church - Joshua 2

I. Set up the story.

II. Why did they choose her house?

III. What do we know about her spiritual condition?

IV. What did she know about God?   v. 9-10

V. How did she respond?   v. 11

VI. For what did she ask?   v. 12-13

VII. Did she keep the matter to herself?

VIII. How was her response remembered historically? Hebrews 11:31

IX. How did her response play out?   James 2:25

X. Did she believe the promise?   v. 17

XI. Think about the scarlet thread.   v. 21

XII. She knew the conditions.   v.18-20   Everyone should know the conditions.

XIII. What did her faith yield?   6:22-25

XIV. Has this changed?   Ephesians 2:8-9

XV. How did her faith affect her family?

XVI. How was her life affected?   Matthew 1:5

Rahab's Church - Joshua 2

I. INTRO
- JOSHUA.
- JERICHO.
- SPIES.
- PICTURES SALVATION.

II. WHY DID THEY GO THERE?
- UNNOTICED.
- PERHAPS GOD DIRECTED THEM THERE.
- "THEY SHALL FIND ME WHEN THEY SEEK ME"

II. SHE WAS A SINNER. ROMANS 3:23
- SHE SAW THEM ENTER – ISRAEL GATHERED.
- PERHAPS HER *CULTURE* DIDN'T THINK SO.
- GOD ONLY SAVES SINNERS.

III. SHE WAS UNDER CONDEMNATION.
- DESTRUCTION COMING. DEUTERONOMY 7
- JOHN 3:18-19

V. SHE KNEW OF THE STORY OF GOD. (40 YEARS) V. 9-10

VI. EVERYBODY KNEW, ONLY SHE SOUGHT DELIVERANCE.

VII. SHE BELIEVED. V. 11

VIII. WHAT A CONFESSION. V. 11

IX. SHE ASKED FOR GRACE AND GOT IT. V. 12-13
- SHE THREW HERSELF ON GOD'S MERCY.

X. SHE WAS NATURALLY CONCERNED FOR HER OWN.   V. 12-13

XI. SHE BELIEVED NOTABLY.   HEBREWS 11:31

XII. SHE PROVED HER FAITH BY WORKS.   V. 1-7, JAMES 2:25

XIII. STANDING ON THE PROMISES.   V. 17

XIV. SCARLET THREAD.
    PASSOVER.
    IN ADAM'S DAY.
    ALWAYS ABOUT THE BLOOD.

XV. SHE KNEW THE CONDITIONS.   V. 18-20
    HEARD THE MESSAGE LOUD AND CLEAR.

XVI. THE SCARLET THREAD FROM ADAM TO CALVARY.   V. 21

XVII. SHE WAS DELIVERED FROM JUDGMENT.   6:22-25

XVIII. HER FAMILY WAS SAVED BY FAITH THROUGH HER.   EPH. 2:8-9

XIX. HER LIFE TOOK A TURN.   MATTHEW 1:5
    MOTHER OF BOAZ, HUSBAND OF RUTH, MOTHER OF JESSE, FATHER OF DAVID.

XX. HARSH WORD "WHORE".
    MEN RARELY CONFESS SIN - ADAM, EVE.
    JESUS IN PARABLES.

        LORD BE MERCIFUL TO ME A SINNER.
        PRODIGAL SON.
        DAVID – PSALMS 51.

SOFT CONFESSION, PERHAPS WE SHOULD ACKNOWLEDGE SIN.

Why Are The Laborers Few? - Matthew 9:35-38

DO NOT HAND OUT THIS LESSON. INSTEAD, ASK THE CLASS TO HELP YOU MAKE A LIST OF REASONS. IT WILL BE FUN AND THEY MAY COME UP WITH SOME GREAT IDEAS. USE THIS LIST ONLY IF THEY DO NOT INCLUDE THEM.

I. In what areas are the laborers few?

II. No Faith.   Hebrews 11:6

FAITH IS A PART OF SHARING FAITH AND SERVING GOD. DO YOU BELIEVE "I WILL BE WITH YOU TO THE ENDS OF THE EARTH"?

III. Unbelief in Hell.   Mark 9:43-48

SEE "BELIEF IN HELL" CHARTS.

IV. Disobedience.   Matthew 28:19-20

FROM THE GARDEN OF EDEN UNTIL NOW - DISOBEDIENCE.

V. Cares of this world.   Matthew 13:22

PROSPERITY IS A MAJOR DISTRACTION. COMPARE BY COUNTRIES.

VI. Too shortsighted.   II Peter 1:9

CAN YOU SEE BEYOND THIS LIFE?

VII. Self-centered.   Matthew 8:21

"SELF" IS PROBABLY THE DEFINING SIN IN THE GARDEN OF EDEN.

VIII. Lack of memory.   Psalm 40:2

FROM WHERE DID YOU COME?

IX. Misplaced priorities.   I Corinthians 15:13

THIS CHANGES EVERYTHING.

X. No vision.   Proverbs 29:18

WHAT DO YOU LIVE FOR?

Belief in Hell by Age

	Age 18-29	Age 30-44	Age 45-59	Age 60-74	Over 74
Absolutely not	8% 22	12% 61	9% 43	12% 33	14% 17
Probably not	17% 46	15% 77	17% 78	13% 37	17% 20
Probably	21% 56	19% 98	21% 98	17.2% 46	17% 20
Absolutely	53% 140	53% 269	51% 229	56% 151	51% 60

Fasting

THIS CLASS CAN BE CONDUCTED IN A DISCUSSION MANNER. NO HANDOUT THIS TIME.

Judges 20:26 Then all the children of Israel, and all the people, went up, and came unto the house of God, and wept, and sat there before the Lord, and **fast**ed that day until even, and offered burnt offerings and peace offerings before the Lord.

WHAT ELSE WAS HAPPENING AS THEY FASTED?

1 Samuel 7:6 And they gathered together to Mizpeh, and drew water, and poured it out before the Lord, and **fast**ed on that day, and said there, We have sinned against the Lord. And Samuel judged the children of Israel in Mizpeh.

2 Samuel 12:16 David therefore besought God for the child; and David **fast**ed, and went in, and lay all night upon the earth.

2 Samuel 12:21 Then said his servants unto him, What thing is this that thou hast done? Thou didst **fast** and weep for the child, while it was alive; but when the child was dead, thou didst rise and eat bread.

2 Samuel 12:22 And he said, While the child was yet alive, I **fast**ed and wept: for I said, Who can tell whether God will be gracious to me, that the child may live?

WHAT WAS DAVID HOPING FOR AS HE FASTED?

2 Chronicles 20:3 And Jehoshaphat feared, and set himself to seek the Lord, and proclaimed a **fast** throughout all Judah.

FASTING IS PRIVATE BUT CAN BE MADE PUBLIC.

Ezra 8:21 Then I proclaimed a **fast** there, at the river of Ahava, that we might afflict ourselves before our God, to seek of Him a right way for us, and for our little ones, and for all our substance.

WHY WAS THIS FAST PROCLAIMED?

Psalm 69:10 When I wept, and chastened my soul with **fast**ing, that was to my reproach.

WHAT INTERNAL AFFECT WAS HAD BY THIS FAST?

Daniel 9:3 And I set my face unto the Lord God, to seek by prayer and supplications, with **fast**ing, and sackcloth, and ashes:

WHAT WAS DANIEL TRYING TO GAIN BY FASTING?

Matthew 4:2 And when He had **fast**ed forty days and forty nights, He was afterward an hungered.

WHY WOULD JESUS FAST?

Matthew 6:16 Moreover when ye **fast**, be not, as the hypocrites, of a sad countenance: for they disfigure their faces, that they may appear unto men to **fast**. Verily I say unto you, They have their reward.

WHEN, NOT IF?

Matthew 6:18 That thou appear not unto men to **fast**, but unto thy Father which is in secret: and thy Father, which seeth in secret, shall reward thee openly.

WHAT BENEFIT IS LINKED TO FASTING?

Matthew 9:15 And Jesus said unto them, Can the children of the bridechamber mourn, as long as the bridegroom is with them? but the days will come, when the bridegroom shall be taken from them, and then shall they **fast**.

Matthew 17:21 Howbeit this kind goes not out but by prayer and **fast**ing.

WHAT KIND?

Luke 18:12 I **fast** twice in the week, I give tithes of all that I possess.

WHY DID THIS PHARISEE FAST?

Acts 13:2 As they ministered to the Lord, and **fast**ed, the Holy Ghost said, Separate me Barnabas and Saul for the work whereunto I have called them.

BAM! NEW TESTAMENT FASTING.

Acts 14:23 And when they had ordained them elders in every church, and had prayed with **fast**ing, they commended them to the Lord, on Whom they believed.

HOW LONG DID THEY PRAY?

1 Corinthians 7:5 Defraud ye not one the other, except it be with consent for a time, that ye may give yourselves to **fast**ing and prayer; and come together again, that Satan tempt you not for your incontinency.

NO FOOD, NO SEX, SELF DENIAL! GOD HAS MORE FOR YOU THAN YOU IMAGINE.

Talk Intentionally

"If you alter or obscure the Biblical portrait of God in order to attract converts, you don't get converts to God you get converts to an illusion. This is not evangelism, but deception."
-- John Piper

A message is hard to deliver without words. We all have heard that Francis of Assisi said, "Preach the Gospel at all times and, when necessary, use words." The implication is that every believer should LIVE a Godly life. No one argues the efficacy of right living. However, other people besides followers of Jesus live moral and even generous lives. Most Muslims are fairly moral, and they certainly have a hospitable nature that emanates from their culture. Asian people are very respectful and helpful people. Mormons are famous for taking care of people and helping meet their needs. SO, if your life seems to be a model life with concerns for the well-being of others, are you Muslim, Mormon, Asian or Christian?

When the Gospel was first given to the Gentiles, it was given to a very moral and upright man, Cornelius, Acts 10:

> *"There was a certain man in Caesarea called Cornelius, a centurion of what was called the Italian Regiment, [2] a devout man and one who feared God with all his household, who gave alms generously to the people, and prayed to God always."*

Unfortunately, this man was lost. Had he died, he would have gone straight to hell. He lacked something, Acts 10:4:

> *"Your prayers and your alms have come up for a memorial before God. [5] Now send men to Joppa, and send*

> *for Simon whose surname is Peter. ⁶ He is lodging with Simon, a tanner, whose house is by the sea, He will tell you what you must do."*

We know what he was told to "do" from the end of the chapter. He was given the Gospel and was told to accept Jesus, which he did.

There is a marvelous reason that Jesus is called the "Word" in John 1:

> *"In the beginning was the Word, and the Word was with God, and the Word was God. ² He was in the beginning with God."*

Jesus was the communication from God to men. Without the "Word" we would not, could not, understand what God wants us to "do."

All of that said, let it be known that sooner or later, some conversation must be used to give the message of Jesus. For some reason, many believers feel that it is unacceptable to use spiritual talk. I find it refreshing that some of our famous TV personalities use language that mentions God. I have heard Jay Leno say, "God bless you." Drew Carry quite often says, "God bless you." Muslims always say, "En shaa Allah" (if God wills it). Why is it that "followers of Jesus" gag on the words that "out them?"

The Bible has much to say about our speech. Good or evil can proceed out of the mouth. Helpful or destructive messages can be spoken.

2 Samuel 23:2

The Spirit of the Lord spoke by me, and His word *was* on my **tongue**

Psalm 5:9

For *there* *is* no faithfulness in their mouth; their inward part *is* destruction; their throat *is* an open tomb; they flatter with their **tongue**.

Psalm 10:7

His mouth is full of cursing and deceit and oppression; under his **tongue** *is* trouble and iniquity.

Psalm 12:3

May the Lord cut off all flattering lips, *and* the **tongue** that speaks proud things,

Psalm 12:4

Who have said, "With our **tongue** we will prevail; our lips *are* our own; who *is* lord over us?"

Psalm 15:3

He *who* does not backbite with his **tongue**, nor does evil to his neighbor, nor does he take up a reproach against his friend;

Psalm 35:28

And my **tongue** shall speak of Your righteousness *and* of Your praise all the day long.

Psalm 37:30

The mouth of the righteous speaks wisdom, and his **tongue** talks of justice.

Psalm 51:14

Deliver me from the guilt of bloodshed, O God, The God of my salvation, *and* my **tongue** shall sing aloud of Your righteousness.

Psalm 119:172

My **tongue** shall speak of Your word, For all Your commandments *are* righteousness.

Psalm 126:2

Then our mouth was filled with laughter, and our **tongue** with singing. Then they said among the nations, "The Lord has done great things for them."

Isaiah 50:4

The Lord God has given me the **tongue** of the learned, that I should know how to speak a word in season to *him who is* weary. He awakens me morning by morning, He awakens my ear to hear as the learned.

Psalm 19:14

Let the **words** of my mouth and the meditation of my heart be acceptable in Your sight, O Lord, my strength and my Redeemer."

Include spiritual language. It should be common vernacular for believers to use words like God, blessed, praise, praise the Lord, God bless, amen, and Bible. Have we let the secular world scare us into their shell? We have bought into the idea that people will think less of us. Yesterday I met a believing Egyptian businessman. He has shared his faith with thousands in Egypt under the penalty of death. In America, we risk very little, but mostly aren't willing to risk anything. Stop being ashamed of your faith.

Pick your spots. As previously mentioned, people will reveal their hearts and needs as they speak. A wise believer will listen to what people are saying and can offer spiritual solutions. We are told in Hebrews 4:16:

> *"Let us therefore come boldly to the throne of grace, that we may obtain mercy and find grace to help in time of need."*

Since God designed life so we would need Him, perhaps another person's need is God ringing them up. By listening carefully, you will be able to pick your spots better.

Leading comments. One day I heard a teenager say, "I've never been to church." I viewed the statement as a request for information. I knew that the mom, a single mother, was always trying to do the best thing for her child. I approached the mom one day and suggested that her child seemed to have some unanswered questions, spiritually. I offered to go to their home and teach a series of Bible lessons that would help them both get answers. She agreed, and I spent 12 weeks in a weekly meeting, and both of them accepted Jesus as their Savior. Listen well, serve well.

Avoid religious statements. Some believers love religious sound bites ("God is in control", "Jesus is the answer", "Jesus saves", "God said it, I believe it", "God didn't create Adam and Steve", "I'm not religious but spiritual"). It doesn't matter if these statements are true or not; they don't explain anything to an unbeliever. People need compassionate, lovingly-delivered information. Sound bites are annoying and generally repel the lost. They do not draw them.

Avoid antagonism, confrontation or probing questions. Do I really need to say this? YES! Some people act like they have no sense at all. You should never criticize someone's religion. It only makes them defensive. If you force someone to justify his religion, you have lost the war. It's better to say, "I think that all religion makes us kind of divided. It never draws people together. I prefer to simply quote the words of Jesus about the matter. Do you mind if I do that?" Can you see the difference between that and "Your religion teaches falsehoods?" Come on! This is not rocket science.

Some people like probing questions. I don't like questions that make people uncomfortable. I might like drawing people out by saying, "May I ask you a spiritual question? Where do you stand with God? Where are you on your spiritual journey?" I like that rather than, "Do you know if you died today you would go to heaven?" "Are you a Christian?" Yes or no questions aren't as good as creating a discussion.

I'm also not a big fan of telling people they are wrong. I was recently with some people, and one of them was being rather judgmental. The other man said, "Don't be judgmental." What do you think happened? Do you think that man number one repented? Of course he didn't. We spent the next five minutes listening to him explain why he was not being judgmental. Criticism never works. It only irritates.

Use simple bridge statements. Most people can present the Gospel in some way. The challenge is the first sentence. Once you make the first sentence, the rest is relatively easy. An intentional soulwinner will be armed with several bridge statements that are good for most occasions. Over the years, I have developed several that work for me. Each one can be used with a slight modification.

1. "Do you mind if I share a spiritual idea with you?" Most people will tell you yes.

2. "I know how you feel. I have felt that way myself. I have found that talking to God works for me." What would you say next? Think about it and you will become intentional.

3. "Do you mind if I share some philosophy with you? I have found that life is like a three-legged stool, and you have to pay attention to each one or your stool tips over. The first leg is physical. You must take care of yourself physically or you will have trouble. The second leg is mental. You have to stay well balanced or things won't go well. The third leg is spiritual. This is the one that includes God, and if you need supernatural help, He's there. When you have no place to turn, He has an answer. You can draw from resources that are beyond you. If you would like to include God in your problem, let's first get Him included in you. Then we can both talk to Him together about this matter."

4. "This problem is bigger than me. It is over my pay grade. Let's figure out how to get God involved. What do you say?"

Once a strategically placed bridge statement is made, the rest becomes easy. ALWAYS rethink your conversation later to determine what you could have said better. Practice makes perfect.

Plan Intentionally

"Being busy does not always mean real work. The object of all work is production or accomplishment, and to either of these ends there must be forethought, system, planning, intelligence, and honest purpose, as well as perspiration. Seeming to do is not doing."

-- Thomas Edison

As an associate pastor, my job was to ensure that all first-time visitors were visited, **and** that an aggressive outreach program was implemented. It made sense to me that all people representing the church should be competent to present the Gospel. As a matter of procedure, we began a soulwinning class to ensure that those making follow-up visits could make a sensible presentation of the Gospel. Can you do that?

One day, while on a training visit, I decided to put my trainee into the fray without much notice. I actually knocked on the door, pushed the trainee up to the door, and said, "It's your turn." Wow! Was that enlightening! Even though he had studied the presentation and had appropriately marked his Bible, he suddenly became a fumble bum. As the man of the house answered the door, my trainee began to try to talk. He did so badly that he couldn't identify the top of his Testament. He had a difficult time saying anything that made sense.

For your instruction, there are several things that you can do or learn to make the Gospel understandable to all.

Mark your Bible

I have a New Testament that I have been using for over 30 years. When I first bought the Bible, I marked it to reflect the "Romans

Road." The Romans Road is simply a method of presenting the Gospel using the Book of Romans. Since the Bible is all about the story of redemption, one could use many other passages to present enough Gospel to win the entire world. For this explanation, I will use the Romans Road.

Starting at Romans 3:10, write the reference for the next verse next to Romans 3:10 in your Bible or New Testament.

The reference to write next to Romans 3:10 is Romans 3:23.

At Romans 3:23, write Romans 6:23a.

At Romans 6:23, write Revelation 21:8.

At Revelation 21:8, write Romans 5:8.

At Romans 5:8, write Romans 6:23b.

At Romans 6:23, write Romans 10:9.

At Romans 10:9, write Romans 10:13.

I will explain how to use them in the next section. By writing these references next to each verse, the only reference that you need to remember is Romans 3:10. If you can remember Romans 3:10, you can get started with your presentation, and you'll know where to go from there.

Make clear points

The points that need to be made using the Romans Road are:

1. We are all sinners, and so are you. (Romans 3:10 and Romans 3:23)

2. There is a price tag for sin: death. (Romans 6:23a and Revelation 21:8)

> 3. Jesus paid the price for us on the cross. (Romans 5:8)

> 4. By "believing", He becomes our Savior. (Romans 10:9)

> 5. Tell Him that you are "believing." (Romans 10:13)

It is not enough to simply read the verses. You must tell what point you are making. Tell the listener before you read the verse and tell them *again* after you have read the verse. **Make the point**.

Watch transitional statements

I find that the statements that make the presentation understandable are the transitional statements. The statements I use go something like this:

There are four things that you must believe in order to make the connection with God. First we must believe that we have a need.

> 1. We are all sinners, and so are you. (Romans 3:10 and Romans 3:23)

Not only are we sinners but there is a price tag on sin.

> 2. There is a price tag for sin: death. (Romans 6:23a and Revelation 21:8)

That's the bad news. Now let's hear the good news.

> 3. Jesus paid the price for us on the cross. (Romans 5:8)

If Jesus paid for the sins of the entire world, then who goes to heaven and who doesn't? Religion has many answers to that question. Let's ignore what religion says, and find out what God says.

4. By "believing" He will become our Savior. (Romans 10:9)

If you can believe this in your heart, then let's tell it to Jesus.

5. Tell Him that you are "believing." (Romans 10:13)

Make the presentation

In this section I will try to give the Gospel presentation as realistically as I can. I personally spend some time trying to "make nice." It is important for me to be a regular guy and be liked by the listener. I also feel strongly that my presentation should not seem "canned." I promise that it IS "canned", but practiced well enough so as not to SOUND canned. I will call my listener 'Joe'.

Here we go.

Joe, there are four things that a person must believe in order to make a connection with God. When I say "believe", I will qualify that in a minute. I'm actually talking about a very serious and sincere kind of belief.

The first thing that you must believe is that we have a need. One usually can't be helped until they admit that they need help. The Bible tells us in Romans 3:10 that "there is none righteous no not one." Righteous means in right standing with God at all times, and the Bible tells us that no one is like that. In fact, the Bible goes on to say in Romans 3:23 that "all have sinned and come short of the glory of God." Sins are those shortcomings that we all have that violate the heart and righteousness of God. Simply put, we don't measure up to God's standard. Therefore we must acknowledge that we are sinners. I'm a sinner, you're a sinner, we are all sinners. Do you agree with that?

The next thing that we must believe is that there is a penalty for sin. In Romans 6:23(a), we are told "the wages of sin is death." It places a price tag on sin. We all understand wages, don't we? Wages are something that we earn. For sin we earn death. But death is more encompassing than we generally think. In Revelation 21:8, we are told about the "second death." The first death is when the body dies, and the second death is when the soul dies forever in the "lake of fire." For simplicity let's just call this hell. So the full price for sin is death, and death in hell. That doesn't sound like a place where I would like to go. How about you? Now that's the bad news.

Let's see if we can find some good news. In Romans 5:8, we are told "but God commended His love to us in that when we were yet sinners, Christ died for us." So God, knowing that we were under the penalty of death because of sin, sent His Son, Jesus, to die for us. He died in our place. He died instead of us.

For me that provokes a question. If Christ died for the sins of the entire world, then who goes to heaven and who doesn't? Religion has much to say about that. In fact every religion tries to approach that question. The problem with religion is that is it man-made. How can **man** tell us the way to God? Shouldn't we be listening to God on this matter? Let's see what God says through His Word.

In Romans 6:23(b) it says, "the gift of God is eternal life through Jesus Christ the Lord." It tells us that God wants to give us something called "eternal life." Here we must understand about the gift. How does one get a gift? A gift is something purchased by someone and offered to another. In order for us to get it, we must make a choice. Do I want it or not? Here is the choice: accept the gift of God, eternal life, or reject it and go to hell. Which way would you choose? I choose eternal life; how about you? But how do I receive this gift? What are the mechanics of actually receiving this gift?

In Romans 10:9 we are told "that if you will confess with your mouth the Lord Jesus and believe in your heart that God has raised Him from the dead, you will be saved." It seems to me that we *must* understand what this verse means. Let's look at it phrase by phrase.

First, "if we confess with our mouth the Lord Jesus." This tells us *in whom* to believe. Do you believe that Jesus is the Son of God? Say it. (Most all responses are YES.) That puts you automatically in the minority. Most of the world will not say that.

Second, "and believe in your heart." That qualifies the *kind* of belief that God requires. We must believe more strongly than a mere surface belief; it must be heartfelt sincerity.

Third, "that God has raised Him from the dead." This tells us *what* to believe about Jesus. God has raised Him from the dead. It tells us that Jesus conquered death. What is our problem? The wages of sin is "death." This Scripture tells us where we can go to solve that huge problem. We can take it to the only one who has demonstrated the ability of overcome death, Jesus.

Fourth, "you will be saved." This tells us the *results* of our belief. We will be saved. That's why Jesus is the Savior, one who saves us from something. In this case, He saves us from the penalty of sin, which is death, death in hell.

That's what we all want--to have a Savior Who can help us with this awful condition, and help us make the ultimate connection with God. Jesus is the Savior. Does that make sense?

Since this is the only logical choice, we must take our choice to Jesus and tell Him. Romans 10:13 tells us "whosoever shall call upon the Name of the Lord, shall be saved." It is up to us to take our decision to Him and tell Him that we "believe" and that we accept Him, trusting Him to be our Savior.

This is my basic presentation using the Romans Road. I have used this presentation to win several thousand people to Jesus. This is NOT the only way to present the Gospel, but this one has worked over and over again for me. BUT fishing is only fishing when we gather the fish.

Video Helps

For help with presentations, visit www.seekerministry.com.

Fish Intentionally

"Many men go fishing all of their lives without knowing that it is not fish they are after."
-- Henry David Thoreau

"Look at where Jesus went to pick people. He didn't go to the colleges; he got guys off the fishing docks."
-- Jeff Foxworthy

I have been enjoying watching a reality TV show about fishing in the Bering Sea. Boy, these guys are serious about fishing. Whether fishing for crab or fish, the entire program looks really serious. Another program shows men fishing for giant tuna. They fight for long periods of time to get the fish into the boat. They do this for a living. Each tuna can yield several thousand dollars each, at market. These guys are fishermen!

When I was a kid, we lived near a lake. I had a little rod and reel and a small tackle box with a couple of bobbers, sinkers and a few hooks in it. I even had a couple of lures. How could the fish resist! I used to spend time standing on a dock and casting out 20 or 30 feet with my high-tech equipment. Man, that was the life! The trouble was that I NEVER caught anything but little 4- or 5-inch blue gills. How boring! I can remember lying on the dock, dropping the line and hook between the boards on the dock, and trying to hook one of the little devils. I could actually see them about a foot under the water. They would come up to the bait on the hook, put it into their mouths and then spit it out. Pretty exciting huh?

As I think back to those days and compare to the tuna fishermen, I see a correlation with soulwinning. I was totally green, unprepared, impatient, unwilling to pay my dues and absolutely unsuccessful. I usually ended my small experiences by throwing the worms into the water, and walking away frustrated. The fish had outplayed me.

One thing I noticed with the tuna guys is that they spread blood and meat chunks over the area where they hoped to catch fish. They call this "chumming." It is supposed to draw fish to the area where the boat is cruising. Back to the correlation. This reminds me of some believers' attempts to lure in the lost. It seems to me that most lame attempts to share faith can simply be categorized as spiritual "chumming" in hopes that the "fish" will jump into the boat. I can see why believers give up the idea all together. They walk away, frustrated.

Jesus called Peter, James and John to follow Him. They were fishermen. Jesus told them that He would make them "fishers of men." He mentored them for three years trying to get them equipped to turn the world upside down. For some reason, Peter decided to "go fishing" after the resurrection. He influenced some of the other Apostles to go with him. They had a fruitless night with their OLD profession, John 21:

> *"4 But when the morning was now come, Jesus stood on the shore: but the disciples knew not that it was Jesus. 5 Then Jesus saith unto them, Children, have ye any meat? They answered him, No. 6 And he said unto them, Cast the net on the right side of the ship, and ye shall find. They cast therefore, and now they were not able to draw it for the multitude of fishes. 7 Therefore that disciple whom Jesus loved saith unto Peter, It is the Lord. Now when Simon Peter heard that it was the Lord, he girt his fisher's coat unto him, (for he was naked,) and did cast himself into the sea. 8 And the other disciples came in a little ship; (for they were not far from land, but as it were two*

hundred cubits,) dragging the net with fishes. ⁹ As soon then as they were come to land, they saw a fire of coals there, and fish laid thereon, and bread. ¹⁰ Jesus saith unto them, Bring of the fish which ye have now caught. ¹¹ Simon Peter went up, and drew the net to land full of great fishes, an hundred and fifty and three: and for all there were so many, yet was not the net broken. ¹² Jesus saith unto them, Come and dine. And none of the disciples durst ask him, Who art thou? knowing that it was the Lord. ¹³ Jesus then cometh, and taketh bread, and giveth them, and fish likewise."

DON'T THINK FOR A MINUTE that this experience is about fish. I think that it is about their NEW fishing profession, fishing for men. I think that they are convicted about their straying. Later in the same chapter, Jesus would ask Peter if he loved Him more than "these" (fish).

I have found that in my own life I need to build in a good fishing venue. Over the years I have found that I am most fruitful if I don't leave personal evangelism to chance encounters. Some of the ideas that I have used are listed below.

Door-to-door

I heard a pastor say recently that the day for door-to-door soulwinning is over. I reject such an idea. I DO acknowledge that door-to-door is very hard core witnessing, and not for the faint of heart. I DO NOT, however, think that it is dead. In fact, Jehovah's Witnesses still do it fearlessly. There ARE several nuances that I have learned while practicing door-to-door witnessing.

1. ***Most people are polite***. I have been patronized, dismissed and challenged, but have never encountered anger, loudness or

violence while going door-to-door. At worst, I have been rejected. However, one day while visiting door-to-door in an apartment building in inner city Detroit, my brother-in-law, Gerland, and I had a bad experience. We knocked on a door and a young woman opened the door and said, "Get lost." She then closed the door. Well, that was enough for me, so I began to walk away. Gerland, however, said, "That wasn't very nice", and he knocked on the door again. The young woman came to the door again and repeated her statement. This time she slammed the door loudly. Again I started away when Gerland said again, "That was really rude", and he knocked on the door again. This time a man came to the door with an ax handle in his hand. I *knew* that I was ready to leave! Gerland, however, felt that he should try to engage him in a conversation. SLAM WENT THE DOOR! Finally Gerland realized that this would not bear fruit, and we left. WHEW! That experience was BOTH of the times that the door was slammed in my face while doing door-to-door soulwinning. It probably could have been avoided. What do you think? Incidentally, I still have never gone door-to-door WITHOUT someone accepting Jesus. It is ALWAYS fruitful.

2. *You must develop a script.* It is very difficult thinking on your feet under a pressure situation. You must predetermine what your opening statement will be and rehearse it. I have found that you have about five seconds to make a case for being given another five seconds. You must quickly identify yourself, and tell what you are doing on their porch. Perhaps you could offer a brochure or a pamphlet. Perhaps it could advertise the church, or some benefit to the resident of the home. Most people want to know only one thing while deciding to entertain an unexpected guest, "WIIFM" (what's in it for me). A perceived need must be presented such as "We are just inviting people to church" (perhaps they have a felt need to attend church). I developed a script that mentioned an invitation to church, but quickly shifted

to the gospel. By handing them a tract with the church info on the front, I could then say, "By the way, inside it tells you how you can know for sure that you are going to heaven when you die. I guess we all care about that, don't we?" Their reaction to that question would allow me to know how to proceed. If they responded positively to that question, I would withdraw the tract and say "I'm somewhat of a specialist in that area. May I share with you how that works?" The response lets you know where to go from there. *A predetermined script is an absolute requirement.*

3. ***You must be thick skinned.*** The easiest way to do that is not to take anything personally. The people you may encounter don't know you. If they **knew** you, they would probably learn to like you. You **personally** will not be rejected. Your visit may be. Perhaps you have interrupted something. Remember, your visit is unexpected. Simply be nice, follow the script, and don't expect to be invited into every home you visit. It just won't happen. In fact, you may only find one in ten people who will welcome your visit. Just remember that Jesus Himself spent three years in public ministry, demonstrating miraculous power, feeding and healing thousands, even raising the dead, but only 300 people were found in the upper room on the day of Pentecost. Honestly, going door-to-door is exhausting emotionally. Most people can't divorce themselves from the rejection.

4. ***It is empowering.*** If you ever do door-to-door soulwinning for any length of time, it will lift your confidence level through the roof. Your boldness quotient will forever be raised. It will make witnessing to your friends and family almost easy, having succeeded at *hard core evangelism.*

Bus ministry teaching/Sunday School teachers

Aggressive bus ministries do not still exist as they did in the 70s. I'm sure that some churches still offer to pick up people for church, but the aggressive evangelistic ministry where people are receiving Jesus by the droves does not exist today. However, I am convinced that the principles used then can still be used now through the Sunday School. I think that any Sunday School teacher can pick up neighborhood kids in his car and take them to church. *Anyone* can win a fifth grader to Jesus. Maybe it's not as challenging as winning a drug dealer, but it can have as big an impact in the cosmic scheme of things. In fact, it may prevent a child from turning *into* a drug dealer.

If a child is entrusted to a neighbor (you) to be taken to Sunday School, it creates an open door to win the parents. Simply by dropping by and telling the parents, "We know that every parent cares what their kids are taught in Sunday School." Entrance can be made into *any* home at *any* time. I did this years ago when I was a bus captain. My wife, Jeanette, and I used to pick up a hundred kids a week for Sunday School. I would spend all day Saturday rounding up kids, and then we would pick them up on Sunday. On our bus we had a driver, navigator, stewardess, captain and a musician (my wife played the accordion). This was a well-oiled machine (INTENTIONALITY). While using information I gathered on Saturday, I would let the navigator know at which homes to stop. The navigator would sit behind the driver and convey the directions. The stewardess would help maintain order on the bus and get information from the new kids. My wife would play the accordion and lead singing. I was free to oversee the entire thing. I enlisted the help of a bus mom on the route to call ahead to get the kids up as the bus was coming. It seems that the parents didn't always care enough to get the children up on Sunday. Hundreds of kids accepted Jesus.

On Tuesday and Thursday evenings I would get a partner and go visit the parents. As I was greeted at the door, I would say, "Hi kids, tonight is for parents." Of course, I knew the parents by then, having picked up their kids for some time. I would tell them, "We know that every parent cares what their kids are taught in Sunday School, and tonight we are here to share that with you." We were always let in and always given a hearing. What parent in his right mind would say, "I don't care what you teach my kids"? They were obligated to listen. We discussed some of our methods of teaching, assuring the parents that we only taught the Bible, not religion. We then told them that the main thing that we taught was how to get to heaven when we die. After giving the details of the Gospel, many parents accepted Jesus themselves. Hundreds were saved.

This approach could work an*y time* that a Sunday School teacher decided to use it. Every Sunday School teacher should do this. In fact, you don't even need to be a teacher. Just pick up a neighborhood child and take him to Sunday School.

When the late Jerry Falwell started his ministry while in college, he was given a class of fifth grade boys. In the church where he attended, they didn't have a room where he could meet with his class. In fact they didn't have any fifth grade boys for him to teach. They *did* find him a space in the furnace room where he could teach (don't tell the fire marshal). He began to find fifth grade boys in his neighborhood. After a short while his Sunday School leaders were forced to find a room for him. Not long after that he had 200 fifth grade boys. Can you imagine how many parents he would win through those kids? The rest is history.

It is my opinion that this method is the absolute easiest method of reaching people for Jesus.

Chaplain

Even though not everyone can be a Corporate Chaplain, I feel that I should mention this as a venue that has been very fruitful for me. I spent five years as a Corporate Chaplain through Corporate Chaplains of America. My task was to see every employee every week to offer any spiritual help that they might need. I actually saw 700 employees every week who worked for six different companies. It was not as difficult as it sounds to engage 700 employees. Most of the time, the greeting was a simple, "Hi, how are you doing today? Is everything okay with your family? Can I do anything for you today?" Usually it only took a minute or two for this brief encounter.

Having pledged confidentiality, I was regularly drawn into employees' life issues. It could be anything from illness to marital problems, from drug issues to a family death, from trouble with the law to premarital counseling. It was common to spend only minutes with an employee but just as common to spend a couple of weeks with an individual and his family, trying to solve a problem.

I adopted the idea that a problem was an open door for me to introduce Jesus into the situation. In Hebrews 4:16 we are invited to "come boldly to the throne of grace, that we may obtain mercy and find grace to help in *time of need*." Since that offer is made to us, why should we try to solve "needs" without including Jesus? I found it very easy to bridge (BRIDGE STATEMENTS) from the problem to Jesus. It only seemed natural for me to say, "This problem is over my head; let's see if we can get God involved. But before we do that, let's get God involved in you; then we can approach Him together about this issue." Most people involved in a life conflict are very open to drawing on supernatural power.

As a Chaplain I was involved in many weddings and funerals. Both of them were high yield for salvations. Each will be discussed below by itself. It is quite possible to make a tasteful and appropriate presentation of the Gospel during both weddings and funerals. All told, I saw 650 people come to Jesus during my five years as a Corporate Chaplain. Around 150 of the 650 came regularly to Bible studies. It was a good time for evangelism and discipleship.

<u>You may not be able to become a Corporate Chaplain</u> but some of these evangelistic ideas can be used by anyone who regularly interacts with other people, perhaps at work or in the neighborhood.

Man of peace

Luke 10:5-7 tells us about a man of peace. This person is a help to those trying to follow the Great Commission, evangelizing the world. A man of peace is a person who has some influence and will allow our "soulwinner" the opportunity to interact within that circle. Depending on that person's credibility, many can come to Jesus. There are several ways that I have used the influence of a man of peace in my evangelistic ministry. By the way, there is no reason to limit yourself to one man of peace. At this writing I am working with 12 men of peace. Each one opens up a new horizon for lost people.

1. **New converts** are a great resource for more new converts. In John 4, after her conversion, the "woman at the well" went back into the city testifying, and many of the people of that city believed on Jesus. Years ago, while pastoring, several new converts in my church caught the vision of reaching their friends and families. One lady brought 40 people from her circle all on the same Sunday. Many of them received Jesus that day and others were led to Jesus in their homes on follow-up visits.

Another lady convert caught fire for Jesus and ended up serving in the bus ministry. She was responsible for bringing hundreds to church and to Jesus. One of my stories mentioned earlier in the book was of a man and wife saved during my personal neighborhood visits. They led me to dozens of people who accepted Jesus. _Never underestimate the value of one new convert._

2. **A business owner** can be an incredible resource for evangelism. If they will let you into their business either to hold Bible studies or to personally visit with employees, people will come to Jesus. It has been my great privilege to serve several businesses as Chaplain. Hundreds came to Jesus. In my opinion, Christian business owners have a stewardship responsibility to share the Gospel with their employees. Perhaps the employees have no interest, but should at least be given the opportunity to decline. The vast majority of the world has never had the blessing of making that choice. It seems to me that a business owner should allow a person to come into their business, offering the opportunity to employees to hear the Gospel. The owner probably shouldn't try overtly to win his employees personally because of the "owner/employee" relationship. It would be very awkward and may even cause legal issues. As I write this paragraph, I am encouraged to go find a business owner.

3. **A seasoned Christian** can also be a wonderful "man of peace." Unfortunately, most believers do not, or will not, try to reach their friends and families (PHILOSOPHY). They will, therefore, have unreached family members, friends or neighbors. The older a Christian gets, the fewer lost friends he will have. Most seasoned Christians will find their associations in church and never try to reach anyone. They grow content and complacent among the "brethren." They love going to church, prayer meetings where they pray for sick church or family

members. The closer they get to death themselves, the more conscious they become of their own mortality, and they seem to sink into a pattern of measuring their lives by how many surgeries they have had. To me this is a pitiful state. They seem happy enough, but are missing the real joy that God has for those who partner with Him in reaching souls for Jesus.

If, however, they get inspired to see the lost saved, they can put you into a vast pool of lost people. They probably won't try to win them themselves, but they will cheer for you as you do. It seems that one should try to come along side of these folks. They won't take much convincing but they will need inspiring. If they do sign on to become a "man of peace" they will find a renewed zeal and purpose for life. Nothing is more exciting to me than visiting the nursery where souls are being born into the Kingdom of God.

4. **A pastor** has more influence than most. He can become a true man of peace by hooking you up with *all of the above*. I served as a missionary in Portugal for two years. One prominent pastor put me on the map quickly. He was more interested in "Kingdom" work than most. By that, I mean that he could see the value of people being saved and discipled regardless of whether or not the convert came to HIS church. In my opinion, many pastors have an imbalance in their thinking toward their own church *building*. I have even known pastors who would discourage some of their best workers from answering the call to ministry, in order to keep them in their own churches. I certainly understand that kind of thinking, but don't subscribe to it.

If you want to win souls, go to your pastor and ask him if he could connect you with a businessman, new convert or a seasoned Christian with a Kingdom mindset. He will gladly do it.

Bible studies

What if I told you that you can get lost people to come to a Bible study group? Over the past few years I have developed a method of drawing together "seekers" into small study groups. Some of them have been in the workplace and some in neighborhoods. Several philosophical conditions must be met to make it happen.

1. A **host** of a Bible study must NOT teach his own group. Most people are known by their *context* and not by their spiritual journey. An accountant is not normally known as a Bible teacher. Therefore by enlisting the help of an "expert" (someone with a briefcase that no one knows) to teach the class, "seekers" are more likely to come. Many people will drive half-way across town and pay $100 to hear an "expert" speak on a certain subject, such as real estate investing. By touting the credentials of the teacher, some people will identify with him.

2. **"Low hanging fruit"** will be found somewhere around a believer, assuming the believer is the "right kind." It is impossible to tell what God may be doing in the life of a lost person. At any time a person may be having a personal struggle, and they may be searching for answers. The timing may be just right for them to be invited to a Bible study group where they can find out "how to get God to bless their life."

My father was low hanging fruit when he accepted Jesus. He was having a bad summer because he had three teenage sons who kept getting into trouble (I was one of them). My father realized that he needed some help in his life and the timing was right. When presented the option, he accepted Jesus.

Let our serious believers invite friends, family and neighbors (or workplace colleagues) to a Bible study taught by a specialist as mentioned above. The timing will be right for some.

3. **Take your time** getting to the Gospel. I have developed a series of lessons (www.charlesyoungphd.com) that present the story of redemption in a methodical method. The participant is not given the option of accepting Jesus until the eighth lesson. Almost all of them do. I call this pre-discipleship. By the time the convert is saved, they already have developed a custom of meeting together, praying, and reading the Bible in a small group. There is no reason to stop. Groups that I start just keep going.

4. **Don't worry about the results**. It is God's business to draw sinners. We cannot do God's work. Only He can decide who He wants to save at any given moment. If only one person comes to the Bible study, it is enough. The person could be the next Billy Graham.

5. **Don't criticize any particular religion**. During the first lesson I always tell the group that we will not be studying religion. I say that religion is not invented by God. Religion is the "man-made" set of rules, ideas, dogmas, rituals, do's, don'ts, and practices. All religions make the same claim, they are right and everyone else is wrong. We all know that can't be true. Actually, it is my feeling that religion is my enemy. It becomes a barrier between us and God (PHILOSOPHY). While teaching it is better to say, "We can go directly to Jesus with our prayers" than to say, "You don't need to pray through a priest." The later statement is an attack on some religions. It may be a correct statement, but not necessary to say. It will actually be counterproductive.

6. **Follow the new convert's family.** What a thrill to see a person give his heart to Jesus. An equal thrill is to see that person develop an interest in seeing his family become followers of Jesus. A family coming to Jesus completes the family. Anything less leaves the family incomplete. A new convert's zeal for his

family and his newfound faith is a powerful tool for evangelism. Use it wisely.

Church visitors

A very easy kind of visit to make is to first-time visitors to church. They have already expressed an interest by attending and they probably have some questions. Some may already be believers, and some will be seeking spiritual help.

Years ago I was the Visitation Director of a fast-growing church in Michigan. We would have as many as 100 first-time visitors per week. Most of them were bus ministry people, and many of them were drive-in visitors. It was typical for us to have special promotion days which could draw in as many as 200 drive-in visitors on any given Sunday. My task was to see to it that these people were visited on a timely basis. I enlisted the help of some good people who, after some training, did a great job with these follow-up visits. I personally made a large portion of these visits per week. Hundreds of people were led to Jesus during those fruitful days. I learned some tremendous truths during that time that have served me well over the years.

Even though a visitor may already have a church background, I never assume that they are saved. So as not to insult, I change the diagnostic questions that I ask a church person. I might ask them, "How long have you been a believer." This is a soft question that does not sound "diagnostic." A follow-up statement could be, "Tell me about that experience, I would love to hear it." It won't take long for you to learn of their salvation or the lack of it. Even if they tell me of a reasonable salvation experience, I might then ask, "Did it take?" meaning did it actually make a difference in your life. I have had some actually tell me "no."

For those people who don't actually have a church from which they are visiting, I might ask, "What is your religious background." That gives me some frame of reference for our discussion. I also like to ask, "What made you come to church now?" This may reveal a need in their lives. Even though I have asked the question, "If you died today, would you go to heaven?", I don't particularly like it. It seems too intrusive. Over the years I have concluded that the Apostle Paul, after his conversion in Acts 9, may not have answered that question correctly. His issue was not "going to heaven" but instead it was, "Who is Jesus?" When he answered that question correctly from the heart, he was converted. I prefer the question, "How do you stand with God?" It is not a yes or no question, and requires some thoughtful answer. If they have been saved, they will tell you. If not, they will also tell you.

By the way, I never call ahead before stopping by. In these days of voicemail, you may never get to talk to them anyway. Phoning ahead gives the visitor too many outs from the visit. It also seems most likely that you will get permission to visit a church member from another church, but NOT get in to see non-believers. I *always* drop in for the visit and say, "I just took a chance that this would be a good time to stop by; could I take just a minute?"

Business networking group

I joined a business networking group, and spent about 2 years attending every Thursday morning. I was allowed to make a "pitch" every meeting. I began by saying "I am Charles Young, and I'm a minister. I help people connect with God without the confusion of religion." The appeal was very provocative. It intrigued them. One benefit of being in this group was the one-on-one meeting that was required of every member. I would spend an hour with each person. I would listen to their presentation about their product or service, and then I would present mine. It became very fruitful. From these meetings I was able to start 5 or 6 groups, and won 25% of the entire group to Jesus.

Prison ministry

I could never have dreamed of the success of a prison ministry. We started by having a teaching class once a month. It evolved into a worship service once a month with the prison praise team. From there, we began to teach a seminary class with a dozen students. I taught the students to reach out into the prison. Other prisoners accepted Jesus as a result of the efforts of the students. I made the students the personal workers at the monthly worship service. They became the spiritual resources for the prison. We also started a seeker group which evolved into a discipleship group. In all dozens and dozens accepted Jesus as we reached 30% of the prisoners in the prison. Some prisoners were transferred to other prisons where they actually began their own ministries. A prisoner with a life sentence has very little purpose in life UNLESS he becomes a minister that reaches his fellow inmates.

In addition

Other venues that have proven fruitful to me were funerals, weddings, premarital counseling and marriage counseling. Details for making these ideas fruitful can be found in *Charging Hell with a Squirt Gun*.

Back to the subject of venue

Regardless of the venue you choose, it is not likely that you will consistently win people to Jesus unless you find a venue where you can serve. Don't worry about being comfortable. It has never been about your comfort. I think that God wants us to always be stretching ourselves. Jesus certainly wasn't comfortable at Calvary.

What are you doing, chumming or fishing?

Follow the pattern of the serious fishermen, and get prepared for the harvest.

Intentionally Drawing the Net

"We are all in the business of sales. Teachers sell students on learning, parents sell their children on making good grades and behaving, and traditional salesmen sell their products."
-- Dave Ramsey

Most believers who share their faith (not many) are usually content to chum and not fish. I think that a person is only "fishing" if they actually plan on "landing the catch." It seems that most people are afraid to actually press for a decision because they might get rejection. Nobody likes rejection! This fear is probably the greatest reason that most believers don't win souls.

Interestingly, soulwinning and sales are quite similar. Anyone who learns to win souls effectively would probably make a good salesperson and vice-versa. I remember a saying about copy machine salespeople. They go "out the door, door to door, floor to floor, 'til there ain't no more." It sounds like a tough job, but those people learn some mad sales skills as they try to make a living. What they learn is that being nice to people works. You never have to be obnoxious. You never have to be pushy. THAT'S what soulwinners need to learn. It is not being pushy or obnoxious.

Years ago while a pastor, my secretary had a Fuller Brush salesman who visited periodically at her office at the church. As her boss, I didn't mind because it wasn't intrusive. She would often buy something from his catalog. Whenever the salesman came, I would give them plenty of space to visit. I would usually leave them alone as I didn't want to intrude. I did notice that the man seemed to be a little mousy sort of guy. I didn't find him very impressive. I actually told my secretary what I thought of him. It wasn't meant to be mean, just an observation. One day, I decided to meet the man when he came for a visit. What I found surprised me. In just a few minutes I had a catalog in my hand and he was showing me something that he thought might be of interest to me. I bought a tie rack. HOW COULD THIS HAPPEN? I didn't intend to buy anything. How did this little mousy guy for whom I had no respect, talk me into buying a tie rack? He didn't try to sell me a toilet brush. He noticed that I was wearing a tie. He spoke to MY desires. He had some skillful language. He had honed his skills, and was good at what he did. CAN YOU DO LESS WITH ETERNAL MATTERS? It is worth your efforts to get good at this.

Our salesman asked me, "Do you have a tie rack?" He asked me, "How many ties do you have?" I have learned some language that helps me to engage people without being pushy. I always try to be nice and respectful. I always try to observe body language that might be negative. I always listen to what I am told. I always listen for "hot" topics in the person's life. I always ask questions to determine their level of interest.

It is my opinion that every person should have the privilege of saying, "No." Too often, we assume that they are not interested and would say no anyway. Shame on you! It's easy to say "Where are you in all of this?" or "What do you think?" or "Does this make sense?"

Give your testimony

I always give my testimony at this point. My testimony helps the listener to relate to me, what I did and the decisions that I made. Here is the testimony that I use to relate to the listener:

Here is what happened to me. I went to a Bible study group to be with a girl. Little did I know that the material presented would make sense to me. I expressed interest in learning more, and a man took me aside to share with me. He explained these same things to me that I have explained to you. He showed me from the Bible that I was a sinner. That was not news to me. I knew of my own mischievous nature. He showed me the penalty for sin. I didn't like that much, but there it was in the Bible. He told me that Jesus died me for on the cross. I was amazed but grateful. He showed me that if I would believe in Jesus that He would be my Savior. It made sense to me and I wanted to do it. Then he asked me a question. He said, "Do you want to go to Heaven when you die?" I have thought of that question many times since. He did not ask me what religion I wanted to be. He didn't ask me if I wanted to go to church. Instead he asked me about my eternal destiny. I answered YES. Then he asked, "Could I pray for you?" I couldn't see any reason to say no. Then he said that he would stop in the middle of his prayer and help me to "call on the Lord" asking Him to save me. I was glad that he offered. I wanted to, but didn't know what to say.

We bowed our heads and prayed and he helped me to tell Jesus that I wanted Him to save me. When it was over I looked around expecting something to be different. Nothing was. Everything looked to same to me. I thought surely something should change. It took me some weeks or months to realize that there *was* a change, but that it was INSIDE ME. My heart had changed. I have never been sorry that I accepted Jesus as my Savior. I could never have imagined the pathway it would put me on. It has been an amazing journey.

Assume the best

Is presenting the Gospel any different from any other presentation which asks for a decision? People are generally fearful about making decisions about anything. Even though this is the greatest decision they will ever make, it may be the easiest. Don't assume that they need to think about it. Don't assume that they must weigh the issues. We already know that they should accept Jesus. We know that there is no down side to it. JUST MOVE AHEAD AND LEAD THEM TO JESUS.

Throughout the presentation we have been asking for little agreements on each sub-issue. The prospect does not need much more convincing at this point. Too much convincing may talk them out of it. Don't try to talk them out of making the big decision. Assume the best!

Draw the net

After making my presentation and after giving my testimony, it is time to draw the net. Drawing the net is a fishing term where the fish are actually collected in the net and pulled into the boat. Since we are "fishing for men" drawing the net is an applicable term.

This is when I say,

"May I ask you the same question that was asked of me?" (Always answered yes.)

"Do you want to go to heaven?" (Yes.)

"Then let me make the same offer that was made to me; may I pray for you?" (Yes.)

"I will stop in the middle of my prayer and lead you in a simple prayer helping you ask Jesus to be your savior." (Don't wait for a response.)

"Remember, prayer must be from a sincere heart. The best you can, try to be sincere."

"Let's bow our heads and pray."

Lead in prayer

"Dear Jesus. Thank you for dying on the cross for us. Thank you also for Joe's interest in connecting with You. Please help him today to be sincere when he asks You to save him." Now Joe, with our heads bowed and eyes closed repeat this prayer with me and be as sincere as you can. "Dear Lord Jesus, I know that I'm a sinner." ………… "I'm sorry for my sin." ………… "The best I know how, I accept Jesus as my Savior." ………… "I know that I can't save myself." ………… "So I'm trusting Jesus as my Savior." ………… "I need you in my heart." ……….. "I need you in my life." ………… "I need you in my family." ………….. "Please be my Savior." ……….. "In the name of Jesus, amen."

The birthing room

I was in the delivery room when both of my children were born. Each time I found myself weeping. I can't really tell you why, but I was weeping. Perhaps it was the idea that one more person came out of the room than went in. Perhaps it was the miracle of birth. Perhaps it was in gratitude that everyone survived the experience. Maybe it was just relief. It could have been joy over one more tax deduction. **Who knows!** I can only say that it was an amazing experience.

When someone opens his heart to Jesus, it is a similar experience. New life has been given. It is greater than physical life. It is a life that will live forever. It is a life that will meet you in heaven. It is a life that will reach fulfillment here on the earth as well as final fulfillment in heaven. It will put a person and possibly a family onto the path that God intended for us all. It is the new birth spoken of in John 3. *It is a miracle.*

Pray Intentionally

"When we rely upon organization, we get what organization can do; when we rely upon education, we get what education can do; when we rely upon eloquence, we get what eloquence can do. And so on. But when we rely upon prayer, we get what God can do."
-- *Dr. A. C. Dixon*

Have you ever been in a prayer meeting? What do most people pray about? I find that most believers pray for health, relationship matters, travel mercies, finances or wayward children. It isn't bad that these are matters for prayer, but these all have one thing in common: they are temporary matters. It seems to me that we should pray for more *eternal* matters. One fix for this issue is to hand out a prayer list that asks for names of lost people. As a pastor, I would always ask during prayer time for people who were thinking about someone who was lost, for salvation. At least they had the opportunity to think about the lost. I believe the issue is a responsibility of the leadership of the church/class/department or group.

<u>We should pray for opportunities</u>. While a missionary in Portugal, my wife and I prayed one morning that God bring someone across our path that needed Him. We left our apartment and got on the subway to head into town. As we talked with each other, a lady in the next seat was listening to us. She engaged us, and in no time we were in a deep conversation about life, ours and hers. We all got off of the Metro at the same stop, and continued our conversation on the loading dock. We talked for half an hour. Toward the end of our conversation, I told her that my wife and I had prayed for God to lead us to someone today that He wanted to bless, and that it "looks like you're it." She

looked stunned! I then said, "Let's explore this and see what God has in mind for you." She thought she was interested in what God wanted for her. In a short while, she accepted Jesus as her Savior.

Following that day, we spent a lot of time together. She accompanied us to several Bible study groups, and became good enough to actually teach a group. It all started by us praying for God to lead us to someone. Have you ever tried that? Perhaps our Sunday School classes could prosper in soulwinning if we changed our prayers.

<u>We should pray for specific people.</u> One Sunday evening at church, my wife and I responded to the sermon which challenged us to have a daily family prayer time. We made the commitment to pray together daily. *That one thing has been a real struggle for us over the years.* We never officially stopped doing it but we have restarted many times. Our individual pace and temperament have made shared prayer a struggle for us. As easy as it sounds and as beneficial as it is, I regret that we have been largely unsuccessful in that practice.

On the next Monday morning, after our Sunday evening commitment, we met together to pray before we both went to work. As we bowed our heads, I let Jeanette lead in prayer. While she was praying aloud, I was praying silently. For some reason Bill and Sue were in my mind, and I was praying for them to become Christians. *Imagine my surprise when I heard my wife pray for Bill and Sue.* **Hey! I was also praying for them.** When it became my turn to pray aloud, I, too, prayed for Bill and Sue. Both Jeanette and I shed tears for them that morning. When the prayer time was over I suggested that if we were going to pray for them, we should go see them. We both agreed. We decided to drop by their house the next Thursday evening. We went unannounced in order not to create any anxiety or questions about our visit.

When we got there, we were welcomed into their home. They were always very cordial people. We began by telling them that we were concerned for them, and we wanted to share with them our faith. They already knew that we were very active in our church. I gave them the plan of salvation. It was accompanied by tears from Jeanette and me. At the end of my presentation, I suggested that we "take care of this matter." Sue began to share with us an inner desire to know God. She told us that just the other day she had said to Bill, "I think that we should become Christians." My wife immediately wanted to know when that was. Sue said, "Monday morning." (Give me a here minute to wipe the tears from my eyes.) **Monday morning!** That was when Jeanette and I had prayed together for them. That was when God put it into their hearts. They both bowed their heads and accepted Jesus as their Savior.

It's a good thing. Can you see the value of praying for the lost? Pray intentionally.

Conclusion

"People who don't believe in missions have not read the New Testament. Right from the beginning Jesus said the field is the world. The early church took Him at His word and went East, West, North and South." -- J. Howard Edington

"I have but one passion: It is He, it is He alone. The world is the field and the field is the world; and henceforth that country shall be my home where I can be most used in winning souls for Christ." -- Count Nicolaus Zinzendorf

"The Church exists for nothing else but to draw men into Christ, to make them little Christs. If they are not doing that, all the cathedrals, clergy, missions, sermons, even the Bible itself, are simply a waste of time. God became Man for no other purpose." -- C. S. Lewis

"The Great Commission is not an option to be considered; it is a command to be obeyed." -- Hudson Taylor

"It is the duty of every Christian to be Christ to his neighbor." -- Martin Luther

"If your Gospel isn't touching others, it hasn't touched you!" -- Curry R. Blake

"How you believe God perceives people will determine how you respond to them." -- Jacquelyn K. Heasley

"Some wish to live within the sound of a chapel bell; I wish to run a rescue mission within a yard of hell." -- C.T. Studd

"I have but one candle of life to burn, and I would rather burn it out in a land filled with darkness than in a land flooded with light." -- John Keith Falconer

"We talk of the Second Coming; half the world has never heard of the first." -- Oswald J. Smith

"As long as there are millions destitute of the Word of God and knowledge of Jesus Christ, it will be impossible for me to devote time and energy to those who have both." -- J. L. Ewen

"The spirit of Christ is the spirit of missions. The nearer we get to Him, the more intensely missionary we become." -- Henry Martyn

"We Christians are debtors to all men at all times in all places, but we are so smug to the lostness of men. We've been "living in Laodicea ", lax, loose, lustful, and lazy. Why is there this criminal indifference to the lostness of men? Our condemnation is that we know how to live better than we are living." -- Leonard Ravenhill

"Someone asked 'Will the heathen who have never heard the Gospel be saved?' It is more a question with me whether we -- who have the Gospel and fail to give it to those who have not -- can be saved." -- Charles Spurgeon

"It is now possible to live a "Christian life" without doing the things that Jesus commanded us to do. We have hired people to go into all the world, to visit those in prison, to feed the hungry, to clothe the naked, to care for widows and orphans. The average Christian doesn't have to do it." -- Cal Thomas

"Sympathy is no substitute for action." -- David Livingstone

"Tell the students to give up their small ambitions and come eastward to preach the gospel of Christ." -- Francis Xavier, missionary to India, the Philippines, and Japan

"In the vast plain to the north I have sometimes seen, in the morning sun, the smoke of a thousand villages where no missionary has ever been." -- Robert Moffat

"No one has the right to hear the gospel twice, while there remains someone who has not heard it once." -- Oswald J. Smith

"Missionary zeal does not grow out of intellectual beliefs, nor out of theological arguments, but out of love." -- Roland Allen

"Use your ministry to build people, not people to build your ministry." -- Jacquelyn K. Heasley

"Give me one hundred preachers who fear nothing but sin, and desire nothing but God, and I care not a straw whether they be clergymen or laymen; such alone will shake the gates of hell and set up the kingdom of heaven on earth." -- John Wesley

"If you are walking with Jesus, in the Spirit, you need not fear going too far. No believer has gone as far as God wants him to go." -- A. A. Allen

"'Not called!' did you say? 'Not heard the call,' I think you should say. Put your ear down to the Bible, and hear Him bid you go and pull sinners out of the fire of sin. Put your ear down to the burdened, agonized heart of humanity, and listen to its pitiful wail for help. Go stand by the gates of hell, and hear the damned entreat you to go to their father's house and bid their brothers and sisters and servants and masters not to come there. Then look Christ in the face -- whose mercy you have professed to obey -- and tell Him whether you will join heart and soul and body and

circumstances in the march to publish His mercy to the world."
-- William Booth

"He is not seeking a powerful people to represent HIM. Rather, He looks for all those who are weak, foolish, despised, and written off: and He inhabits them with His own strength."
-- Graham Cooke

"God uses people. God uses people to perform His work. He does not send angels. Angels weep over it, but God does not use angels to accomplish His purposes. He uses burdened broken-hearted weeping men and women." -- David Wilkerson

"If we are devoted to the cause of humanity, we shall soon be crushed and broken-hearted, for we shall often meet with more ingratitude from men than we would from a dog; but if our motive is love to God, no ingratitude can hinder us from serving our fellow men." -- Oswald Chambers

"I don't know how your theology works, but if Jesus has a choice between stained glass windows and feeding starving kids in Haiti, I have a feeling he'd choose the starving kids in Haiti."
-- Tony Campolo

"While women weep, as they do now, I'll fight; while children go hungry, as they do now I'll fight; while men go to prison, in and out, in and out, as they do now, I'll fight; while there is a drunkard left, while there is a poor lost girl upon the streets, while there remains one dark soul without the light of God, I'll fight-I'll fight to the very end!" -- William Booth

"Great opportunities to help others seldom come, but small ones surround us daily." -- Sally Koch

"As a large fire begins with kindling of small twigs and branches, even so a large revival is preceded by the prayers of a few hidden seemingly insignificant souls." -- Gary Amirault

"Every man is a missionary, now and forever, for good or for evil, whether he intends or designs it or not. He may be a blot radiating his dark influence outward to the very circumference of society, or he may be a blessing spreading benediction over the length and breadth of the world. But a blank he cannot be: there are no moral blanks; there are no neutral characters." --Thomas Chalmers

"To silence a preacher from preaching judgment is like being awoke from sleep by a fire alarm, and just silencing the alarm, and going back to sleep." -- Unknown

"If you teach men that God is the source of their pleasure and sin is the source of their pain, they will run to God and away from sin." -- Jacquelyn K. Heasley

"Evangelization is a process of bringing the gospel to people where they are, not where you would like them to be... When the gospel reaches a people where they are, their response to the gospel is the church in a new place." -- Vincent Donovan

"God has huge plans for the world today! He is not content to merely establish a handful of struggling churches among each tongue, tribe and nation. Even now He is preparing and empowering His Church to carry the seeds of revival to the uttermost ends of the earth." -- David Smithers

"We must be global Christians with a global vision because our God is a global God." -- John Stott

"Have you no wish for others to be saved? Then you're not saved yourself, be sure of that!" -- Charles H. Spurgeon

"I believe that entertainment and amusements are the work of the Enemy to keep dying men from knowing they're dying; and to keep enemies of God from remembering that they're enemies."
-- A.W. Tozer

"We should be more concerned with reaching the lost than pampering the saved." -- David McGee

"A schoolmate of Matt Chandler's with the locker next to his: "I need to tell you about Jesus. When do you want to do that?"
-- Matt Chandler

"It is the great business of every Christian to save souls. People complain that they do not know how to take hold of this matter. Why, the reason is plain enough; they have never studied it. They have never taken the proper pains to qualify themselves for the work. If you do not make it a matter of study, how you may successfully act in building up the kingdom of Christ, you are acting a very wicked and absurd part as a Christian."
-- Charles Finney

If not you, who? If not now, when?

Made in the USA
Charleston, SC
27 September 2015